NONI JABAVU

A Stranger at Home

Introduced by
Makhosazana Xaba and
Athambile Masola

Tafelberg

Tafelberg
An imprint of NB Publishers
A division of Media24 Boeke (pty) Ltd
40 Heerengracht, Cape Town, 8000
www.tafelberg.com
© 2023 Noni Jabavu, Makhosazana Xaba and Athambile Masola
Columns reproduced with permission from Arena Holdings

Set in Merriweather
Cover image: Amazwi Museum Collection
Cover design Michiel Botha
Book design by Nazli Jacobs
Edited by Eugenie du Preez
Proofread by Kathy Sutton

Printed by *novus print*, a division of Novus Holdings

First edition, first impression 2023

ISBN 978-0-624-08936-0
ISBN 978-0-624-08937-7 (epub)

For

Virginia Phiri who from 1999 facilitated Noni's final return to South Africa and later accompanied her from B C Leon Home in Harare to Lynette Elliot Frail Care home at no. 23 Allenby Road, East London on 05 May 2002.

Tembi C. Mbobo who organized and led a team of women writers who welcomed Noni at the O R Tambo airport in Johannesburg while Noni and Virginia were on transit to East London.

Alexandra Hope Notemba's sons – Tengo Xhosa and Benedict Carter – Noni's grandchildren, without whom this book would not be possible.

CONTENTS

INTRODUCTION

This book is a compilation of columns written by Helen Nontando (Noni) Jabavu for the *Daily Dispatch* newspaper in East London in 1977. It is a significant slice of history and a project against the erasure and flattening of Black women's identities. Noni's writerly identity — one of many she had — is remarkable, considering the way women were often presented in public discourse during her lifetime.

Society's need to see women through narrow, confining lenses and roles as mothers, wives and carers/nurturers has been shifting over the decades as women have been adamant in claiming and owning their wholesome and complex selves. Noni's books, *Drawn in Colour: African Contrasts* (1960) and *The Ochre People: Scenes from a South African Life* (1963), were published by John Murray in London and St Martin's Press in New York. An Italian translation of *Drawn in Colour* came out in 1962 in Italy. Noni was a memoirist of the 1960s, becoming the first Black South African woman to publish memoirs. She also became the first Black person, the first woman and the first person born outside Britain to edit *The New Strand*, a literary magazine. She edited five issues at the magazine's London office from December 1961 to April 1962, at which point she moved to Jamaica. The *Daily Dispatch* columns are the first of her writings that were published in South Africa, making her work readily available to the South African reader. *The Ochre People* was later reissued in 1982 by South African publisher Ravan Press.

Who were Noni's peers in the South Africa of the 1960s, when she was editing *The New Strand* magazine? Nicolette Ferreira provides a useful entry point. In *Grace and the Townships Housewife: Excavating South African Black women's magazines from the 1960s*, Ferreira notes:[1]

> Between 1965 and 1969, most politically orientated magazines produced by the Black press in South Africa were silenced as a result of apartheid's restrictive measures. This was, however, a time when Black women's magazines could become more prominent, as they were viewed by the apartheid government authorities as apolitical and thus less of a threat to their political agenda.

The 1960s witnessed the birth of two magazines: *Grace* (October 1964–December 1966) and *The Townships Housewife* (February 1968–April 1969), which 'appear to be the first women's magazines in South Africa aimed specifically at Black women'.[2] The women who wrote for these magazines were Noni's peers, in her country of birth. Although both magazines were white-owned and driven by profit, they constituted a platform where 'African women express[ed] their needs and aspirations'.[3] Interestingly, there was a letters page in *Grace* entitled 'I write what I like'; readers wrote whatever they wanted to say which 'creates a platform for us to start considering the link between *Grace* and the awakening of Black Consciousness in the early 1960s'.[4] The list of Black women's names continues to point to the need to excavate more writings by Black women, and to demonstrate that the male domination of the Black press in the 1950s and 1960s was not left unchallenged. In one of the chapters, Ferreira makes the following conclusion:

In contrast, then, the 'backward' depiction of Black South Africans in white magazines such as *Die Huisgenoot*, *Sarie Marais* and *Fair Lady*, Black women in *Grace* and *The Townships Housewife* are young, modern, beautiful and glamorous. *Grace* and *The Townships Housewife* challenge the representation of Black women in white women's magazines, while simultaneously disturbing the representation of Black women by a mostly male magazine staff during the preceding *Drum*-decade.[5]

One wonders, did Noni ever read these two magazines? Did any of these writers know about and read Noni's books? More specifically, did Patience Khumalo, the editor of *The Townships Housewife*, ever read Noni Jabavu, the editor of *The New Strand* magazine, and vice versa? Knowing as we do that the deepening and systematic entrenchment of apartheid created walls between people, it is possible that the answer to these questions is a categorical 'no'. That said, it is also possible that the answer is a categorical 'yes' because the written word has the capacity to travel: it can create holes through concrete walls, cross bridges, swim up and down river streams, climb mountains and fly over borders to faraway lands. The written word can be unstoppable.

Patience Khumalo, like Noni, was a pioneer in her editorship of *The Townships Housewife*:

> Patience Khumalo, Black 'editress' of *The Townships Housewife*, deserves acknowledgement for her position as Black female editor of a magazine for women – not even popular Afrikaans women's magazine, *Sarie Marais*, had a female editor until 1994.[6]

11

Grace was the brainchild of Mrs Esther K Nyembezi,[7] who wanted to challenge the way Black women were written about by Black men and white people. The list of names Ferreira excavated through her invaluable research on the two magazines for Black women by Black women deserves a spotlight in this introduction:

> Women who penned stories and articles for these two magazines, such as Zebediela Malifi (in *The Townships Housewife*), Mrs IG Buthelezi, Thandi Zulu, Molly Moreni, Kathleen Mkwanazi, Jo Simpi, Candy Mtetwe, Likhwa CW Mpofu, T Dmbithula, Eileen Sithole, Fato Ngobele and Violet Xolo (in *Grace*), deserve recognition for being part of this new decade of women's magazines.[8]

In 2019, Noni would have turned 100 years old. Born on 20 August 1919, she died on Wednesday 18 June 2008. A few days earlier on a Sunday, I had shared my Noni biography project and journey on a panel called *The Role of Biography in Understanding Our Pasts*. Noni's columns also do the same kind of work – they help us understand our pasts; nomadic, writerly and otherworldly. Her columns were written in a decidedly personal style; what she called 'personalised journalism'. In a letter to a friend in 1978, Noni mentioned her plans to compile her columns into a book. She wanted to revise the columns slightly so that they were less casual and conversational, and instead took on a more narrative and literary tone. The publication of this book is a realisation of one of Noni's dreams.

The *Daily Dispatch* newspaper was established in 1872 under the editorship of Massey Hicks. In 1977 Donald Woods, the editor, had been in this position since 1965.[9] Noni was living in Kenya when she visited South Africa in 1976 for three months; she returned in

July and stayed until December 1977. She was conducting research to write a biography of her father, Davidson Don Tengo Jabavu, popularly known as DDT. Her first column reflects on her experience upon arrival at the airport; how the immigration officers had not believed she was a British citizen. And her retort, 'I became British in my own right in 1933,'[10] had not made her situation easier. This airport experience became her reintroduction to occupying the position of a perpetual suspect, an undesirable, a nuisance and a loud-speaking, know-it-all native. Racism was however not the only challenge that Black women had to face daily. Black men, sometimes in cahoots with white men because of their patriarchal beliefs, were also a hindrance, a marginalising force and perpetrators of women's oppression. Women lived this reality daily, long before the currently fashionable use of the concept 'intersectionality' became a quotable in conversations on feminism.

Who else were Noni's peers in local newspapers? Thenjiwe Mtintso is a well-known journalist who worked at the *Daily Dispatch* in the 1970s. Her illustrious career as an activist and one of the very few women commanders of uMkhonto weSizwe (MK) – the underground military wing of the African National Congress (ANC) in exile – and as a world-renowned diplomat during the democratic era has become legendary.

Other journalists of the 1960s and 1970s – Joyce Sikhakhane, Sophie Tema and Suzette Mafuna – were based in the then Transvaal, working in a male-dominated environment during the apartheid years. Sarita Ranchod interviewed women journalists and published an article, *Herstories Celebrating Pioneering Women in South African Journalism*.[11] Of the women Sarita interviewed, Sophie and Joyce had been in the journalism profession since the 1960s. In 1963, Joyce became the only woman at *The World* newspaper. Nomavenda Mathiane earned her stripes at *The World* during the

1976 student uprisings and subsequently wrote for *Frontline* magazine, focusing specifically on South African townships. Bessie Head, the novelist, became well known for her writings published in *Drum* magazine and in 1963 was the first Black reporter for the *Evening Post*.

Going even further back, in 1957 Juby Mayet, also a short story writer, started writing for the *Golden City Post*, where she wrote reports, features and columns. Later she moved to *Drum* magazine and in 1977 she made history by becoming the first Black woman to be a deputy chief sub-editor at *The Voice*.[12] Other women documented as having written for *Drum* magazine are Mavis Kwankwa, whose article was published in 1952. Marie Kathleen Jeffreys, whose pen name was Hamsie, published her first six articles from 1959 to 1960.[13]

Are there Black women journalists to speak of, before the slight boom of the 1950s? This is the question that will need to be answered as the commitment to unearthing and therefore making visible the work of women gains momentum. For instance, whose names come to mind when we think of the first isiZulu newspaper *Ilanga lase Natal*, established in 1903? When did the newspaper employ the first woman and what role did she play, what did she write about? It has been well over 100 years since *Ilanga lase Natal* began.

We do know that a century earlier Daisy Makiwane, who was an elder sister to Florence Thandiswa Makiwane – Noni's mother – became the first woman to work at *Imvo Zabantsundu*, a bilingual newspaper in the then Cape Province. The newspaper started in 1884 and it was Noni's grandfather John Tengo Jabavu, popularly known as JT, who was the owner and editor of this newspaper, a first for Black South Africa. Daisy took on many journalistic roles at the newspaper before she left the Cape Province to live in the then Transvaal after her marriage. The story of Daisy's pioneering journalism career is, as far as my research goes, yet to be told.

Charlotte Maxeke – South Africa's first Black woman graduate – wrote in the 1920s in isiXhosa for *Umteteli wa Bantu* newspaper on social and political issues as well as church-related concerns. Notably, she was passionately committed to the 'woman question' and modernity, and thus made an indelible contribution when she founded the Bantu Women's League in 1918.[14]

In a gem that is the *Bibliography of African Women Writers and Journalists*,[15] Brenda Berrian has created eight categories for these writers. Instead of calling the seventh category Journalism, she calls it 'Journalistic Essays'. The Black South Africans mentioned in this book, Phyllis Ntantala, Miriam Tlali and Barbara Masekela, were writing journalistic essays for literary journals and magazines before Noni's time at the *Daily Dispatch*.

As a columnist, Noni did not have to be in the offices of the *Daily Dispatch*. She sent her copy whenever it was ready. Her living conditions were however made very difficult by the apartheid laws. She was not allowed, by law, to live for more than three months in any of the homelands. She lived with relatives and friends in the different homeland areas. She spent some time at Rhodes University and in Cape Town. She writes about what this meant for her in the many letters she sent to friends all over the globe. Beyond her 1977 nomadic experience while at 'home', she had also lived a life of constant movement. As you will read in the columns, her travel experience was extensive.

Noni also believed that travelling is unsettling for a woman. In her own words, 'Making homes across continents can be a marriage breaker. That's one of the reasons I have been married more than once.'[16] Noni was in her late fifties when she wrote for the *Daily Dispatch*. She was writing from the experience of many decades.

Which other Black women were travelling and writing about their travels before 1977?

Athambile Masola – my co-introducer and writer of the Afterword for this book – conducted archival research that tells the story of Black women's travels; not only where and when they travelled, but how they wrote about their travels. Masola's essay, *Bantu women on the move: Black women and the politics of mobility in The Bantu World*, is a story of how Black women were travelling in the 1930s, thus further contextualising Noni's own departure from South Africa in 1933. Noni was thirteen years old at the time.

The four women whose travel writing Masola analyses – Miss EP Ngozwana, Mrs William Dube, Gloria Molefe and Mrs Hilda Godlo[17] – were older than Noni and, most importantly, they bear testimony to the complexity of Black women's lives, the role of education and their aspirations as well as their agency, features rarely associated with Black women of that time. These four were professionals, teachers and nurses.

The 'Bantu women on the move' section of *The Bantu World* newspaper suggests that it had become impossible to ignore women travellers and writers. Masola further argues in her article that 'mobility is political, economic and racial in character'.[18] This raises the question: how much of the travel writing narratives by Black women is an accessible part of the 21st century consciousness about Black women's lives? The four women's articles tell the story of mobility as an aspect of modernity. Considering that a feature of patriarchy is the control of women's bodies, this extends to controlling their mobility, and these articles contribute to our understanding of how individual women expressed their freedom outside patriarchal norms. Noni, like the four women, was disrupting societal expectations of women's lives.

Besides travel, Noni's columns included the themes of family, identity, love, music, writing, marriage and of course apartheid. Unapologetically middle class, Noni made sure that her story lives on by giving glimpses of her life and travels. She was also writing her autobiography, provisionally entitled *Life and Loves of an Ochre Lady,* and therefore not telling it all – yet.

The 1970s were tumultuous times for women in journalism. An extensive quote from Joyce Dube gives a good sense of the times. She writes:

> The '70s saw a new breed of female journalist who faced tear-gas, bullets, detention, police harassment and other atrocities by the Nationalist Party Government. As media workers they worked side by side with their male colleagues, fighting for liberation[s], striving for unionism, sacrificing themselves for the freedom of the press and literally risking their lives for this industry.
>
> Some battles were won – like recognition of unions. Some were lost – when publishers decided to promote journalists, they empowered males as if women could not lead newsrooms. This created a wave of departures from the disgruntled '70s women journalists. Gifted and brilliant writers quit the profession en mass [sic] – Suzette 'Stray Bullet' Mafuna, Matilda Masipa, Pearl Luthuli, Maud Motanyane and many others – to start their own businesses, study or venture into different fields.[19]

This exodus of women from their chosen professions bears testimony to the unbearableness of conditions within newsrooms. These journalists were walking away from being sidelined, marginalised and not taken as seriously as their male counterparts. They were standing up for themselves and, by extension, for other women.

In an edited volume *African Foundational Writers: Peter Abrahams, Noni Jabavu, Sibusiso Nyembezi & Eskia Mphahlele* edited by Bhekizizwe Peterson, Khwezi Mkhize and Makhosazana Xaba, published in June 2022, four of the nineteen chapters focus on Noni, thus entrenching her within the broader South African literary historiography[20]. Athambile Masola's chapter, "A Footnote and a Pioneer: Noni Jabavu's Legacy"[21] argues that while she has been erased in varying ways, her own writing is 'evidence of her own attempt to humanise herself and write herself into history'. Makhosazana Xaba's chapter '"She Certainly Couldn't be Conventional If She Tried': Noni Jabavu, the Editor of *The New Strand Magazine* in London"'[22] excavates a slim slice of Noni's writerly life as an editor from September 1961 to April 1962.

The compilation of these columns constitutes another layer of Noni's visibility and legacy that will hopefully ensure that no future writings on her relegate her to a footnote because she was, indeed, one of the continent's foundational writers.

MAKHOSAZANA XABA

JANUARY

ʊᔱᧁ

'What they don't seem to dig is that time is not on their side.'
Using Noni's own words, her commentary on the apartheid regime,
Peter Kenny ended his column which introduced Noni as a weekly
columnist for the year. This is a poignant comment from a writer
who often pointed out that she was not political. The embers from
the fires of the 1976 student protests and the state's response to
them were continuing to glow in parts of the country, and clearly
Noni's understanding of what 16 June 1976 signalled was indeed
the end of the apartheid regime.

The first three titles of Noni's columns, 'Back home again . . .',
'Getting used to colour again' and 'Back to a bank of family', share
two themes: the negative impact of apartheid in the daily lives of
Black people and the meaning of returning home. She wrote in the
first one: 'Since last March, each moment for me down here is a
minor or major trauma.' It was the apartheid regime's policies that
made it impossible for Noni to travel as she wished and live wherever she chose, turning her into a nomad in the country of her birth.

'Home' is clearly not uncomplicated: it is a geographical as well
as a psychological entity, a representation of family and of origins.
Home is also an absence and a memory. Noni writes about how she
had not been back home for a long time, and the anxieties of that
and what was forgotten.

MAKHOSAZANA XABA

1

Noni Jabavu comes home by Peter Kenny

༄

7 JANUARY 1977

Noni Jabavu has returned to South Africa, like Rip Van Winkle, she says, after an absence of 43 years interrupted by only a few short visits.

But she is not here to stay. The remarkable woman with laughing, oak-coloured eyes, who was an oxy-acetylene welder during World War II and is now famous for her writing, will leave again when she has collected material for her book on her father, Prof DDT Jabavu, the academic and prolific author.

She is now in Umtata, gathering material and visiting friends and relatives.

She is a descendant of two remarkable Eastern Cape families. Her grandfathers, John Tengo Jabavu and the Rev Elijah J Makiwane, were part of a deputation of Cape liberals to the British Parliament to protest Union in 1910 when no Black people were consulted. In England the two made friends with English liberals like George Cadbury of chocolate fame, Joseph Crosfield, a millionaire tea magnate who retired at 26 to devote himself to financing Christian missions in China, and CJ Clark, the shoe manufacturer. The three were all related and all Quakers.

The close ties between these English and South African families continued through three generations. Noni married one of their grandsons. She is Mrs Cadbury-Crosfield in private life.

Grandfather John Tengo Jabavu became the first black editor

owner of a newspaper in Africa when he started *Imvo Zabantsundu* in 1884.

In her deep, lilting voice that bears no trace of a South African accent of any type, she described her grandfather as a strong man and a show-off ... He was a powerful writer, a fierce-tempered six-footer and a splendid equestrian. But she considers her other and gentler grandfather, Elijah Makiwane, a better and more persuasive writer.

This distinguished family notched up another first when her father, DDT Jabavu, became the first black professor in South Africa in the chair of Latin and Bantu languages at the University College of Fort Hare.

One of Miss Jabavu's uncles by marriage, Prof ZK Matthews, was the first graduate of Fort Hare and a former pupil of her father's. He later became the first Ambassador for Botswana to the USA.

Among the many eminent pupils of Prof Jabavu were Transkeian Prime Minister, Paramount Chief Kaiser Matanzima, KwaZulu leader Chief Gatsha Buthelezi, and other prominent African leaders who studied at Fort Hare, such as Botswana's president, Sir Seretse Khama and Kenya's Attorney-General, Mr Charles Njonjo.

Of her family background Miss Jabavu says: 'All these accidents of birth have produced people like me, middle class, indeed upper class, for five black generations here in South Africa. Landowners, politicians, educationists, lawyers, doctors and writers. Am I not lucky to be one of them?'

Noni Jabavu's own gifts and her skilled use of them have contributed to the family fame.

In 1933 as a 13-year-old daygirl at Lovedale, Noni was sent to England to continue her education. There she stayed with English family friends, attending Mount School in York and Church of

England College for Girls in Birmingham. Among her classmates was the theatre star, the late Margaret Leighton.

Miss Jabavu was studying music at the Royal Academy when World War II broke out. She trained as a semi-skilled engineer and oxy-acetylene welder, making parts for bomber engines – one of the first women recruited by Lord Beaverbrook into aircraft production.

She married during the war. When her children, a daughter and foster daughter, were big enough to allow her enough leisure, she gradually established herself as a journalist, BBC broadcaster, TV star, and then as a writer in her own right.

Another achievement was her appointment as the first black and woman editor of *The Strand Magazine* [sic] in 1962, following in the footsteps of her Aunt Daisy Makiwane, who as co-editor with her grandfather of *Imvo Zabantsundu* was South Africa's first black woman journalist.

Her first two books to be published, *Drawn in Colour* and *The Ochre People*, are shortly to be succeeded by *Life and Loves of an Ochre Lady*. All are records of her personal experiences in the countries she has lived in, which include Spain, Egypt, West Indies, Mexico, the USA, Canada, Kenya, Uganda and of course South Africa.

Although this youthful-looking widowed grandmother of 57 with an air of English gentry about her has been absent from South Africa for so long, she is still fluent in Xhosa. But she confesses: 'I speak the old-fashioned type. Xhosa is a growing language and has adapted itself a great deal in 40 years.'

The book she is writing on her father is to be called *Portrait of an Ochre Father*. She is arranging to meet as many of his contemporaries as possible during this protracted visit.

Asked: 'Why only a visit? Why don't you come back for good?' she replied, smiling: 'Because my love life prevents me.'

'I am committed by an enduring heart's affection to my very good man friend in Kenya, a "vanilla gorilla", which is local slang for a Kenyan citizen of white origin! An English bachelor of terrific machismo, he takes care of my problems, is my beloved big 6'3", blue-eyed blonde bully. Very rich, if you must know. Fixes my cup hooks himself, services my typewriter, tells me what to do and I obey.

'But,' she says confidently, 'I value the freedom we extend each other. He has allowed me to come down south for research on this book on condition that while here I am to behave. He maintains I am naughty! He has set a date for my return. So that is that.'

During her absence from South Africa Miss Jabavu has missed its physical characteristics, its breathtaking scenery, great mountains, rivers and the extraordinary vitality and ebullience of its blacks, especially their music-making, jokes and joi de vivre.

'Everything Southern African blacks do, they do with unexampled vigour. After all these centuries of oppression, their spirit seems uncrushable. I am proud to be descended from them, to have been born in this lovely land.'

But she adds sadly: 'It has been spoilt only by the authoritarianism of its currently dominating white African "tribe" whose arrogance is making South Africa a sick society. These people know who I mean. What they don't seem to dig is that time is not on their side.'

2

Back home again...

❦

12 JANUARY 1977

'How do you like our country?' That is the question you are asked whenever you have gone to visit or live abroad. And it's a delicate one to answer because it is not wholly welcoming, it is guarded, rhetorical and above all loaded. You have to choose your platitudinous answer with all the delicacy you can command to avoid giving offence where you don't intend any.

'How do you like being back home in South Africa after so long?' This, understandably, is the question I have been asked daily since I came from Kenya in March 1976 for three months, and again from July onwards. But any of my normal feelings of delicacy in answering were blunted outright within an hour of arrival. In answering, the words pop out of my mouth involuntarily, and they are more than loaded – a flurry of bird-shot: 'Like it? Not at all! Since last March each moment for me down here is a minor or a major trauma.'

To clarify, I explain that by saying 'each separate moment' of arrival, I mean the earlier one at Durban docks and the later one at Jan Smuts Airport. Each brought its own distinctive shock of the unexpected: the moment of truth when the stranger comes face to face with the peak-capped immigration officers, those first representatives of the State at your point of entry into a country.

They always put me in mind of Hitler's stormtroopers; I suppose

24

the sight of them makes the traveller feel anxious and guilty for no reason whatsoever.

How they'll interview you as an individual is something you cannot predict, so you don't know how you are going to react: 'It ain't what you do, it's the way you do it,' as the old song goes. A smile on the face between those forbidding epaulettes of authority will relax you, and immediately your reaction is: 'I'm going to like this country,' whereas a chilly or gloomy expression will tauten you, and send your stomach plummeting down to your boots.

As I last visited South Africa in 1955, I may be excused for having forgotten the feel of adrenalin spurting into your bloodstream when a pair of hostile 'South African European' eyes behold you, the nostrils between them quivering as at something the cat brought in. But I felt it again in a flash, on seeing the kaleidoscope of changing expressions on the face of the officer who took my passport from my hand.

I had watched him deal smilingly with the couple who had preceded me in the queue. The couple now stood waiting for me, for as passengers we had become friends during the voyage. And as I was alone (being a widow), they were among those who had come to attach me to themselves for deck games, cards, drinks, laughter, general socialising and joyfulness. We had planned to join forces on some of the sightseeing trips the Purser had suggested to on-going passengers after we had – as he called it in bureaucratic lingo – 'been processed by immigration'; among ourselves, we didn't call it that, we called it 'being done' … use for ribald laughter, need I say, reverting to adolescence!

Later this couple told me how puzzled they had been to see the surly way the man was doing me! They saw him rearrange his face, wipe off the smiles he had bestowed upon them and put on a scowl to bestow upon me. They suddenly wondered what was going on.

This is how my interview went: the officer scrutinised my British passport. Among other details, it says: 'Place of birth, Fort Hare, CP, South Africa, 20 August 1919.'

He put it to one side, held out a hand.

Then with a start, he jabbed a forefinger at an entry, growled triumphantly: 'This doesn't make you British. You're not British.'

'What do you mean?'

'Married in 1951 is no good,' he said scornfully. 'Even if he was British, date is useless. Relevant year is 1949 for eligibility. Ha! . . . Sorry, you can't enter the Republic.'

'Can't enter? Yet born here – what do you mean?'

'You're claiming you're British – falsely, it looks like. Wait over there.' My stomach turned over (that adrenalin!) for he was glaring at me. I glared back but had the wit to jab my forefinger at an entry he seemed to have missed. I said slowly, acidly: 'Excuse me – read here. This previous husband, 1945, was British, see? And in any case,' I heard myself say, 'I became British in my own right in 1933. Forget your 1949!'

The glittering eyes blazed in disbelief. I hurried on for fear my self-control might snap, for by now I was quivering like a catgut. 'When my Dominion of South Africa passport expired my guardians in England were taking me on holiday on the Continent. They took out a British passport for me. Simple as that in those days.' Triumphant in my turn, I suppressed a vindictive inward 'So there', and 'Ha!' . . . The interview had developed into a duel.

He coloured and dropped his eyes. I too, felt a hot flush suffusing my face, for apart from being old enough to be his mother (he didn't look a day more than 35; had probably never heard that in prehistoric days South Africa was a Dominion of the British Empire), all that apart, I was well into the hormonal turmoil of my age group. Whippersnappers like him are supposed to show respect to elderly ladies.

He busied himself re-examining his array of rubber stamps, my passport again and my marriage lines . . . as well he might, for both are well-filled credentials! At last, selecting a rubber stamp, he gave a page of my passport a violent thump, muttering: 'Well, you can't stay in the Republic longer than this, see?' and shoved my things back at me.

I joined my waiting friends. They were white Capetonians, he a World War II South African Army officer, his wife his sweetheart of the war in Italy.

We repaired to their stateroom, I trembling, they concerned. 'What the hell was happening, Noni? You looked like fighting cocks! Sit down.'

I couldn't speak, only handed him my passport while she brought out an ice-bucket and Campari and poured out three glasses. (All of us had laid in supplies in our cabins the day before, because of course, duty-free booze, tobacco and so on are sealed off in port by Customs.)

I begged him to check what the fellow had stamped in my passport. I was too upset to look myself.

Now he became upset. He handed my passport to his wife and broke out into explanations in voluble Italian. Then both looked at each other and exclaimed and swore: 'Mamma mia!' 'Gott!'

He turned to me, took a deep breath and explained that I had been stamped for a 'three-month only holiday visit'. But, he said gravely, he and his wife were surprised because none of their British passport holding friends were given a time limit. They could come freely for as long as they liked; some of them even took jobs if their cash ran out.

We sat reflecting, in silent communion.

At last he said, sighing: 'This is our first real experience of petty apartheid pinpricks, Noni. I'm South African born and bred, but have never met a black South African to make friends with until you. Now I've seen how they treat you. I could wring their bloody necks, excuse language. What a welcome home for you.'

They had said during the voyage as we had come to know each other, how much they'd like me to visit them in their home. I now wondered whether they'd be allowed to have me in their house as their guest. I had forgotten about the Group Areas Act and they, being typical, ordinary, nice people, 'had never really thought, let alone realised, what these apartheid laws mean to ordinary people like us'. We were friends, similar social class, similar interests, belonged to the same lovely land. Yet now we had fallen silent, sombre and sad because we suddenly had to think of ourselves in terms of whiteness and blackness, because South Africa's laws discourage contact and friendship between South Africans of different colours.

She leaned across and squeezed my hand to ask me a question. (Xhosas like me and Italians like her are demonstrative folks. We touch and hug and make a noise.) She asked how I would now be able to write my biography of my father in only three months instead of the unlimited time I had expected to stay in my mother country to do it in.

Her husband murmured grimly: 'The bastards!' That broke the ice, and she and I cracked up laughing. I said: 'Clearly, I have to revise my plans – eh? My book about my father will have to take longer to do. What I could do in these three months I've been graciously allowed to darken the doors of the Republic is to go on with my journal, these impressions of my life and times in various countries, can't I? I'm in another country now here in Durban' . . . (They had read my books in the past, in Italian translation. I had lived in Italy at one time, in Florence, so, she called me 'Firenz' and I called her 'Bologn' – ungrammatical, both of us. (She was from Bologna.) Her husband said: 'Yes, start with your impression of that "Immigration Van der Merwe".' We laughed.

I looked outside. The friendship of these two South Africans was doing its work, oiling my wheels of cheerfulness. Outside, I looked at many others of their – our – country: black, brown, white and felt it in my bones that there was much in store for me in renewed contacts with them. 'Those contacts will surely not all be negative.' I was thinking, for I remembered now, in 1955 when I was last here, some of my best friends had been Boers.

One nasty apple doesn't spoil the whole bag – an Immigration Officer, who did he think he was, compared with the families in the Eastern Cape? So now I smiled. For was I not home again – is there any place like home? No, there is no place like home. My father was away for ten years. I've been away for about 44.

For him, as for me in my turn, to return is an overwhelming experience. Traumatic. He communicated how he felt. In this column, I am trying to follow his lead.

3
Getting used to colour again

৩৫

Last week I described how I felt on arriving back in my mother country by ship in March 1976, at Durban docks on my point of entry into the Republic of South Africa, destinations Umtata, Transkei and finally Middledrift, Ciskei.

And I described how 'separate development', formerly 'segregation', otherwise 'apartheid', petty and major pinpricks knocked me for a six within an hour of arrival.

I hope you read that for I am itching to describe how I quickly recovered from that first trauma, then dived again, then bobbed up, then again fell down. That's what it's like to peep in and out through the barriers of separate development. I have so much to relate and describe about how it affects you, I am bubbling over!

But first, I must describe my other experiences of re-entering my mother country. Not my 'homeland'. I don't have one. I mean it when I say, 'mother country', where I was born, the then Dominion of South Africa, British Empire.

The business of coming home again is a dreadful exercise if you are a native. We used to be called 'natives' when I was young here. And correctly. Now I find people are called blacks or whites or browns. Why? . . . You tell me, bwana! Is it because in a republic everyone must be reminded of their skin colour? Yet in the Republic of Kenya where I live, black people are very, very black, whites very white by comparison and Asians (Indians here) so very brown and beautiful. Yet is there any of this ridiculous, wicked enforced colour consciousness? Whatever colour we are in Kenya, we are conscious only of our social class as individuals. But here, down south, South Africa? Oh my!

My plan on coming 'home' in March was to stay for as long as necessary to gather material from various sources for my projected attempt at writing a biography of my father, Prof DDT Jabavu. I planned to research in South African universities (not excluding such seats of learning as Stellenbosch, Witwatersrand – little did I know that the seats of learning here are grouped by colour).

I planned to visit the special libraries, archives and talk to individuals who had known or been in contact with this famous scion of a famous family. As my father was known and renowned in every corner of this vast land, my project would take quite a time, broken only by long weekends in Kenya.

But if you read me last week (did you read me? 'Over!') you'll recall that to my chagrin, the immigration laws of South Africa blocked my plan. How? Why? Can you guess? No prizes offered. Because – and no need to hold on to your hat – permission to enter varies according to the colour of your skin. The Geneva Convention of the old League of Nations days no longer applies as it did in the prehistoric days when South Africa was a Dominion. (It used sometimes to be called Zuid-Afrika, ZA, do you remember?)

I, being a black (I mean native) was allowed only three months in my native land. So, I had to revise my programme and spend a fortune travelling unexpectedly back to Kenya, my foster-homeland where I am a 'resident' for as long as I like and free to go and come.

How wonderful it was to be back in Kenya, where my roots go down nearly 10 years! Not only because I was reunited with my big blonde Kenyanean [sic] friend, my vanilla gorilla as Kenya citizens of white origin jokingly call themselves, but because after those three months in a separate development colour-based society, to be once again in a non-racial multiracial society was to breathe again!

I had so much to tell everyone about South Africa I bubbled over. They all exclaimed: 'Noni, you look so happy, so beautiful!' I grinned, I smiled; how could I not smile? Compliments don't come at a tickey a dozen!

I replied: 'Because I've been home.'

'But isn't it awful down there, that aparr-thayd?'

'Yes, it's dreadful. But lakini sikiliza...' and I translated into a mixture of Swahili, English, Kikuyu, a line or two of that lovely Xhosa poem by the late Rt Rev JJR Jolobe (another member of my family incidentally) which goes 'Lento ingumntu yint' ehlal' ihlal' igoduke'... I can't really translate it into English poetry.

My friend Robert Graves, one of the greatest English poets as you know, once said to me: 'Noni, you are no poet, my girl. You are an observer. I am not insulting you. An observer is an artist too. You belong in the club of artists, of which there's no higher species in the human race!' Therefore, I can only tell you that JJR's poem refers to that atavistic instinct, the desire, the longing to return to the land of one's forefathers, of one's birth.

Despite the dreadful shocks I had sustained from the petty and major pinpricks of apartheid, I had nevertheless peeped through these colour barriers and had shot through them to my own relations and had seen something of the tremendous changes that have been made in 45 years, 26 years. And to be seen again by my own flesh and blood had been to be 'doctored' by them, revived, enriched, restored. This is another almost untranslatable aspect of a cultural syndrome. I hope my friends and fellow club members Professor Monica Wilson and Mayer, to name but two here down south, will write to the *Daily Dispatch* and confirm publicly that 'uNoni, intombi kaJili, akaxoki.' – Noni, daughter of her father, is not telling lies . . .

Let me just say that that's the reason why I had become 'beautiful'. I'll talk a lot in this column about this doctoring and ritual 'strengthening' and felling of oxen, spilling of blood which we do to reaffirm that our kin are one and indivisible and belong to one another, however long they have been separated. These rituals are 'native' of course.

By my many husbands of different lands, cultures, civilisations, I have experienced other rituals (when in Rome do or observe what the Romans do). For the moment, this week, I must talk about what happened to me when I came back again to the Republic of SA, this time by air.

When I boarded the huge plane in Nairobi, carrying about 200 or 300 passengers, I looked around quickly at the vacant seats. And espied one next to which sat a gentleman whose face I immediately liked the look of. I made a beeline for it, for he looked about the same age group as myself, late fifties. During the long flight we became friends, we chatted each other up. (You'll have noticed that I love talking . . . if I weren't an author, an occupation which disciplines you to be solitary for eight or 20 hours a day, I would no doubt talk far too much!)

Dialogue is good. Ask Mr Vorster whether dialogue is good or not. My next-door neighbour and I dialogued – oh my, how we talked! And what lovely surprises were in store for us both! It turned out that not only was he not my age group – late fifties – he was in his seventies! A lovely man. And he had thought I was in my thirties!

Not only that he was a descendant of a famous South African literary and political family which, three generations back, had been political and literary friends of the famous South African ditto (literary, political) family of which I am a descendant. He was a Cronwright. I a Jabavu. I was not born, not even an apple in my father's eye and my Mr Cronwright on this plane was perhaps a babe in arms when his and my grandfathers were friends: Cape liberals such as Cronwright, Hofmeyer, Jabavu, Rose Innes, Molteno, Schreiner, Merriman, Sauer.

When the plane approached Jan Smuts Airport, passengers were handed pieces of paper to fill in and pamphlets to read and digest. Mr Cronwright and I worked away filling in the forms, very impatient at being interrupted in our talk about our families and their achievements.

One of the questions was: 'What are your reasons for coming to South Africa?'

I scratched away, filling in that I wanted to do research into the lives of my grandfathers, Makiwane and Jabavu, who had been Cape liberals in 19th-century politics, for I was trying to write a biography of my late father, Prof DDT Jabavu.

Also, I had come to put in order the grave of my only brother, who was shot dead by gangsters in Johannesburg in 1955 when he was about to receive his degree as a Doctor of Medicine at Wits University. In March 1976, I had visited my family graves to lay a stone (a South African ritual), and had seen, to my distress, that in the absence of decades of me and my sister (the only remaining children of DDT and 'Magambu'), these graves had not been properly maintained.

I finished filling in my form about the same time as my Mr Cronwright finished his. (You notice? He is 'my' Mr Cronwright by now!) So is my bank manager in London 'my' Mr Murray and my bank manager in Kenya 'my' Mr Dumford; in Umtata it was 'my' Mr Kirkland and in Durban 'my' Mr Dreyer. I'm like that: I love being protected and helped with my accounts by such civilised gentlemen! Why? I am so upper class that to talk about money makes my frontal lobes go blank! I don't understand money at all.

I nudged my Mr Cronwright and he smiled. We sat back and took deep breaths, 'saphefumlela phezulu' (Xhosa), and looked out and gazed at the Transvaal spreading out down below us. Our plane was coming down to land in about an hour or half an hour. We read our pamphlets. 'Welkom in Suid-Afrika! As U 'n inwoner is wat terugkeer, welkom terug in U land!'

Of course, I had to concentrate on the English version of this. In my Mrs Rip Van Winkle generations away from home, I have learned to read and speak only the world languages, French, Spanish, Kiswahili. Other languages such as Xhosa, Afrikaans, Basque, Finnish, Icelandic are interesting indeed, culturally, linguistically, but of no importance internationally. They are nonetheless of an importance of their own, emotionally. In the cosmopolitan world I've lived in for over 40 years, such languages – and what lovely languages they are – don't count. So, I read the English version: 'Welcome to South Africa! If you are a returning resident, welcome back to your country.'

I nudged my Mr Cronwright again and pointed, smiling. 'That's me,' I said, my heart expanding, glowing in an inner smile of joy. We landed, taxied, came to a halt. We filled the reception hall in our hundreds. Mr Cronwright and I were among the first to present ourselves to the immigration officers.

He was quickly dealt with, and we said our goodbyes to each other. I was told to stand aside and wait. I obeyed. I waited. Waited, waited, waited. Hours passed. The queue thinned out. Immigrants mostly, Italians, Greeks, Portuguese, Scots and so on. Now I could see around me better. At every entrance and exit door I saw youths in uniforms, pointing what looked like tommy guns at all of us, waving these weapons around, their fingers on triggers. My heart thumped. Adrenalin, for I got a shock at the sight. What was going on, for heaven's sake? Were those youths soldiers? No, must be police.

I remembered that white police in South Africa are armed. I had forgotten. (You forget or remember selectively over periods of 45 years, 26 years)... Police are armed to the teeth in my Kenya and in the USA too, where my foster daughter and her husband and children live. But I'd never seen them pointing guns at people the way these young kaburu (Swahili language for Boers) were doing.

Some years back, one of my lovers – or was it a husband? – had given me a little pearl-handled gun for my handbag in Chicago (like a small 'parfum pour le sac') and taught me how to whip it out in self-defence and shoot. But had ordered me in his deep south drawl (he was a Southern states 'nigra', very black, great big chap), 'Doan never pine this thang at nobabdy, hear me?' It took me some minutes to understand what he meant – 'Don't point this thing at anybody'. When we talked, our accents so puzzled us, we generally just cracked up laughing!

But now at Jan Smuts I remembered in a flash and realised why I felt frightened. Young boys pointing guns at me, fingers on triggers, good grief! I had arrived during the 1976 Soweto riots and reflected on the results of separate development and Boer domination – sorry, I mean Afrikaner National Party verkrampte Christian power.

I sighed. I couldn't pray. I'm not the praying type. I just went on waiting. My ankles were swelling now. At my age you tend to have circulation problems. The immigration officer kept coming and going behind those closed doors as I stood and waited. There was not a seat on my side of the counter.

Finally, he came out and sat down. Looked at me and beckoned. We were totally alone in this great hall. The khaki-uniformed boys all now pointing their loaded guns at solitary me. I moved nearer to the seated young officer, shifting from one swollen ankle to the other. We conferred.

He said in a low hiss: 'You were here in March to May. Now July you are here again. Why?'

'Is it a crime?'

He caressed the pages of my passport, bent down to study them again, then raised his eyes level with mine and asked: 'Why all this travelling?' His blue eyes narrowed, piercing mine like gimlets: I hissed back, my eyes widening... (in Xhosa language – 'nda-mvulel' amehlo), 'Why do you ask me that? Is it a sin, an offence for a person to travel? To come any number of times to South Africa? I was born here, you've seen that!'

He shifted his position in his chair from left buttock to right. I was very chair conscious. Our eyes still held one another. He murmured: 'Blacks don't do all this travelling. What were you doing?'

Later his attitude changed. 'Pretoria have telexed. They say: "All right, give the lady a six months' visit permit," as you are going to Transkei for independence celebrations.'

So, he handed me my passport. We smiled at each other warmly now. I thanked him. 'Which of these lavatories may I use? I am bursting – which is the black one for Natives Only?' We laughed and he rose to his feet, came out from behind his side of the barrier and showed me the way, saying: 'This is an international airport – there's no discrimination.' My sideways glance showed me that the young policemen at the doors had relaxed their guns, were pointing them down at the floor. I breathed again!

As I powdered my nose in the non-racial ladies, a thought or quotation was trying to worm itself into the frontal lobes of my brain – something about 'easier for a rich man to get through the eye of a needle than to get into heaven'.

For many years, 'heaven' had been to me the country of my birth. To enter it was my dream of passing through its pearly gates. But here I was being practically turned away like a rich man. Indeed, I was 'rich' in the sense that I was in the mansion of my forefathers and had a right to be there. How could it have occurred to me or any other born South African that you may enter only on condition of skin colour, of Group Areas Acts?

Yet when I had returned to Kenya after my earlier three months' permit, the young and very, very black Kenyan immigration officer had ended his routine examination of me by saying with a broad grin: 'Asante sana kurudi, Mama. Mimi na nchi yetu sipata furaha kabisa kuonana tena.' I'm no better at writing Swahili than I am at writing Xhosa. The ever-changing Bantu language orthographies have confused me since childhood, so I play my languages by ear! What he was saying was: 'Thank you mama, for returning to us. I, representing our country of Kenya, am very, very happy to have you back again.'

4
Back to a bank of family

૨ઉૃઈ

26 JANUARY 1977

After the trauma of landing in Durban after years overseas, things got brighter when I got off the ship at East London.

The atmospheres of apartheid are rather like a fog in England: one minute you're driving through, visibility nil, and with heart in mouth, and the next it suddenly clears for a few yards and you nervously breathe again . . .

Several people had travelled many miles to meet my boat – a contingent of relations on my paternal (Jabavu) side from the Ciskei, and of my maternal (Makiwane) side from Transkei.

It was an emotional, atavistic occasion for me and confusing, too, for as always when I've arrived at East London from overseas for some family crisis, there's been what I've described in one of my books as 'a book of human beings waiting there to meet me', and only later has it emerged who was who, which were my relations, which were friends and supporters in our trouble. You don't always recognise people after many years of separation.

This time I recognised only one of the group immediately. That was one of my first cousins. Everyone took turns to hug and buss me on the cheek. I eased myself off to gaze at him. He gazed back. I beheld a mature young man, very handsome, with a smile that gleamed very white. His ears twitched, reminding me of my sister in Uganda.

I had last seen him 25 years back when he was about 18, my late uncle's last-born and dearly loved by my late parents. My heart leapt uncomfortably.

I turned to a very buxom, very old lady standing beside him, beaming toothlessly so that only red gums showed. I wondered who this could be. She fell on my neck exclaiming in Xhosa in a voice I recognised so that before she finished: 'Yu! Nontando mntan'am, nguwe lo?' (My child, is this you?) I realised she was my father's widow, the lady he married years back when my only brother died.

I had flown home for my brother's funeral, as I had flown four years before that when my mother had died.

So, of course I had met the lady, for at my brother's death, she had been among the many women who had appeared as if out of the blue to help cater for the great crowd of mourners who had filled our house. And I had stayed on with my father for a couple of months for he wished to marry the lady, and for me to be a witness. She had changed indeed.

Since my return last year, I've seen scores of people I'd known before my absences from South Africa and have been amazed how some have altered beyond recognition, others not at all, and others, like my cousin, for the better, grown and gained in stature.

Involuntarily I turned to him again; a fine figure of a man. I felt a surge of reassurance in staring at him. Blood speaks, we say in Xhosa, and what culture of whatever 'colour' has not its own expressions for such intangibles?

Let me tell what happened when I stepped ashore at East London. I was at last past the initial barriers of immigration officers. What lay in store at the Customs Shed where I was to be interrogated by customs officers?

It was cold, raining, gloomy, muddy underfoot, but in the shed, the officers ('Europeans' of course – I was reverting to these South

African terms!) were spotless in white drill uniforms ... and smiling. I smiled back guardedly, not knowing what to expect; I'd seen in Durban how a white smile can rearrange itself into a scowl when the owner of a white name (Crosfield) turns out to be black.

One of these Europeans looked at us undisturbed as we trooped in. Then he gestured to the only chair and suggested, in English, to one of the menfolk that perhaps the old lady might like to sit down. We were silent, but I for one felt a tremendous brightening of the atmosphere.

My four suitcases were lifted on to the counter and the two officers greeted me in genial tones as I fumbled in my handbag for my keys. You see what apartheid does to you? I'm having to underline the fact that these white men were treating me and mine with normal respect!

One stepped forward, murmuring the usual things about 'have you anything to declare'? His colleague looked on, with interest, but not a whiff of the gunpowder of hostility could I detect from either of them. It was around now that I felt no need any longer to be suspicious or to continue mentally underlining signs of attitudes.

I was ready to joke now, and waving at all my opened cases, I said: 'Well, I don't think I've packed my Smith & Wesson or any "horse" [heroin] in my toothpaste tube.' Customs officers from Canada to Kenya have initiated such jests with me. These ones were equally cosmopolitan. The one who was doing the talking replied with a chuckle: 'Have you any books though, or picture magazines'?

I stared, collecting my thoughts. His colleague leaned forward amicably and explained laughingly: 'He means pictures of naked women. Girlie magazines. We have censorship here. If you have naughty pictures, it is our duty to confiscate them and report you.'

By now we were all laughing. I said, acting at being scandalised:

'Why should I carry pictures around? Shouldn't I know what a woman looks like with no clothes on? But I do have a couple of books; presents for relatives and friends.'

'Ah – now what are they? Communist? We'll have to check them,' and he helped me extract them, expertly digging them out from among my clothes.

As he leafed through the pages desultorily, he murmured something about the telephone to the office being out of order because of the rain, and he and his colleague conferred about the titles and he was telling the other one to run up and check them, I supposed at where the Index was.

I said: 'I promise you they are not communist. They are not even banned in South Africa. I am the one who wrote them, so I know.'

Their eyes opened and he exclaimed: 'Go on – you wrote them? You're a writer?' And he told his colleague he'd better call so-and-so from up there as well. While the colleague scuttled off, he told me that so-and-so was a great reader, a real bookworm and would be sure to like to meet a writer.

To cut a pleasant story short, the bookworm turned out to have read one of my books years ago, pointed to it and praised it to the skies, was so touched that he put out his hand to congratulate me, saying how pleased he'd be to tell his wife he had met the author. 'Welcome, Noni Jabavu!' he said.

Naturally, I glowed inside. Authors enjoy being acknowledged. You could say we are as vain a lot as any other artists. We enjoy recognition all the more because, unlike singers or actors, we are invisible, we work away in solitude.

While all these pleasantries had proceeded, another 'European' had crept in noiselessly at a door in the corner of the shed on their side of the counter, and had reached over to the opened suitcase nearest to him. He wasn't in uniform. He wore a grubby, greyish mackintosh, was sallow, deadpan, didn't look at us.

On the top layer of my things in that suitcase lay exposed what I use as a 'travelling office' – two wire trays in which I neatly arrange my current correspondence, pencils bound in rubber bands, address books, bits of manuscript, dictionaries and so on.

This man was silently leafing through my address books, then my dictionaries with concentration. I saw him flip pages back to the flyleaf of my English dictionary. My others were a Swahili and a French.

I nudged the relative next to me, winked and motioned by a side-ways glance towards the mackintosh (in Xhosa 'ndagxelesha') and whispered out of the corner of my mouth: 'Who he?' – quoting *The New Yorker's* Harold Ross!

The whispered reply: 'Special Branch.'

I stiffened as if jabbed with a hat pin. 'Great Scott! What for?'

Another nudge. 'Shh!'. And I had to pay attention to the officers, for they had finished with me now and were bidding me goodbye and wishing me a happy visit to my home folks. I noticed how the English they spoke was almost idiomatic, subtly different from English in parts of the world I've lived in.

We set off on the first leg of my journey to my father's house. My party had come in two cars. We were to stop at King William's Town for an hour or so to see another first cousin there, and shop for groceries.

But I didn't look round me much as we went, for I was disturbed by that 'Special Branch' business and demanded clarification and explanations.

'Are we being followed?'

Perhaps, perhaps not. In any case they would be in possession of my destination. I was wondering what he had been studying so hard in my address books and especially in my dictionaries, for heaven's sake!

When I unpacked my case that evening, I turned to the flyleaves and re-examined the notes I sometimes made in my dictionaries.

I was dashed if I could see that I'd written anything criminal, subversive or communist ... I had made a note in my English dictionary of the word 'eldritch', and now recalled that I'd come across it for the first time in my life two or three years back in the United States when I had belatedly discovered that splendid novelist Calder Willingham and had devoured his paperbacks one after the other non-stop, and had found that in every book he had used that strange word which I knew I myself would never, ever find a use for; I had concluded it was a Willingham 'writer's fad'.

I wished mackintoshed SB much joy of the word 'eldritch'.

FEBRUARY

February's columns begin on a political note as Noni writes about her encounter with the Special Branch, 'The Special Branch call'. Noni is nonchalant about the surveillance she is under as she does not think about the threat she poses as someone related to the Makiwane and Matthews families, who were politically involved.

For Noni there seems to be a thin line between her family and the politics of the day, and this is described in the following week's column, 'Smuts and I'. This column is curious as Noni inadvertently describes her family's proximity to power through her father's relationship with 'Oom Jan', General Jan Smuts. Not only does she describe the intimacy between her family and the Smuts family, but she explains how the circumstances of her move to England when she was thirteen years old are intricately linked to her family's bond with the Smuts family.

In the column 'Going native in Mexico' she continues with the theme of travel, describing her experience in Mexico as well as mentioning other places where she has travelled: Jamaica, Trinidad, Nairobi and Uganda.

This month ends with a column which begins: 'I have to write a letter instead of an article – an attempt to answer all the letters, telegrams and invitations you have written me.' The title itself is peculiar – 'All you need is love' – as it is a nod towards a political system that thrives on hate. She confesses to having lived a full life of experiences which she diligently shares with her readers. She

uses her columns to write about politics and family, and sharing
her love life becomes a political issue.

ATHAMBILE MASOLA

5
The Special Branch call

🐍

2 FEBRUARY 1977

I'd been in my old home at sleepy Middledrift for four days when the Special Branch called; I was leaving next day for Umtata to my maternal relations. And as I sat deep in thought in what had been my father's study and was now a hideous double bedroom stuffed with furniture like a junk shop, one of the many children in the house (my stepmother's descendants) came and said: 'Grandmother says to ask your help to talk to these Europeans who have come to visit her.'

In what had been our sitting room I found her with two gentlemen, one tall, clean-shaven, wearing a grey double-breasted mackintosh, the other short, wearing a heavy brown moustache, pebble glasses and a grey double-breasted mackintosh.

The old lady immediately heaved herself up and beseeched me in a sibilant Xhosa whisper: 'As you know, Nontando, I have this knee,' and hobbled off. She had rheumatism or something.

The visitors seemed undecided who should be their spokesman in response to my opening gambits.

When a woman can't think what to say, her best bet is to smile. So, I fell silent, leaned forward and smiled at them expectantly.

Moustache (my stepmother had not introduced them) blushed and said something to the effect that he was an Umtata man on a visit to the Ciskei. At Fort Hare he'd been told about my famous father the professor, been shown the secondary school named after him and had wished to pay his respects to the widow, and was now glad to meet the professor's daughter, who, he understood, had just arrived from overseas.

I smiled away. There were long pauses. Clean-shaven had a go, but the chat began to peter out.

I felt a guilty pity for them and said to help out: 'You must know my relations in Umtata and round about, then. They are a famous family in those parts, eh?'

Moustache brightened, Clean-shaven looked outside at the view which is magnificent, a river valley, beyond it shallow hills backed in the far distance by blue mountains.

'Oh yes, I know them well. And Rev Bikitsha too has returned from overseas, isn't it?'

I told him the equally famous Bikitsha family were friends of ours but weren't related, and I had not known of a Rev Bikitsha. 'Which overseas country has he returned from?'

Moustache reddened. 'Oh, I must be mistaking him.'

I kept quiet.

'But I hear you have relations overseas?' he said.

'That's correct,' I nodded and smiled.

'And your . . . your cousin Ambrose Makiwane, where is he overseas?'

'Ambrose?' He had been one of my politico cousins. I'd last met him at my brother's funeral here at home. 'Is he overseas – not at Umtata? I was looking forward to seeing him. All my Makiwane relations. You know, of course, what a huge family they are. My great-grandfather had 12 children, didn't he? So maybe you know better than I do how many cousins I must have.'

I rose – tired of smiling now – and took a step towards the verandah, and naturally they had to rise too and start being ushered out. Moustache remarked on the view, Mr Clean echoed him.

'I'm going to Umtata tomorrow. I'll greet the Makiwanes for you. They'll be pleased to hear you visited the professor's widow,' and asked his name.

But fumbling with his hat, he perhaps didn't hear for he didn't tell me.

We said our goodbyes.

As soon as their car had disappeared over the hill behind the house, village neighbours ran down to ask: 'What did the Special Branch want?'

'Oh, Special Branch, eh?'

'Yes, they are the Alice ones.' Apparently, everybody knew them and the registration number of their car. Such knowledge is not top secret in small towns and rural areas!

I unexpectedly saw him again a few weeks later in April at, of all places, the Fort Hare graduation ceremony to which I had travelled from Umtata.

Like me, he was in the audience. Forgetting how chilly I'd been before, I waved with a broad grin.

But he quickly 'threw his eyes', as we say in Bantu languages, 'in another direction'.

It is one of my idiocies that I always forget that an 'awkwardness' exists between myself and somebody or other and hail a familiar face like an old chum. I fully deserved his embarrassed snub!

This was not my last brush with this quaintly-behaved secret service.

Back in Kenya at midday, a letter from Umtata told me that two men from Alice had come to greet me but missed me because I had left for Durban the previous day – elusive woman: mustn't they have wondered what nefarious activities she was engaged in?

As before, they hadn't given their names.

Petty apartheid turns even an extrovert like me into an intro-vert. I couldn't help brooding on this cat and mouse stalking I'd been subjected to in my mother country. What was I suspected of? And in any case, how come such ineptitude?

The security of a state is said to be based on the skill of its secret agents. Then, surely, they should matriculate or at least pass Std VI in a paper on Sherlock Holmes, Raymond Chandler or, if these are 'square' nowadays, Gavin Lyall or whoever.

Furthermore, since neither the Ciskei nor the Transkei Essbees tailed me to my knowledge, why should those at South Africa?

Could there have been a hidden code, a clue in my amateur lin-guistic notes? If so, wait until I bone up on the Taal!

6

Smuts and I

❧

How did you come to be sent to England so young? What did you feel about it?

A house called Tsalta, at Claremont, Cape, was where I first beheld and shook hands with the English couple who were to be my guardians in England. That house was where General and Mrs JC Smuts lived. Its name was backwards for 'At last'.

Like a typical black child of those days, at thirteen I was not too well primed about the negotiations that must have gone on between my parents and my prospective loco parentis about the life they were planning for me which, I was to learn in years to come, was to be a practical demonstration of the generations of friendship between the families. I learned then that the plan was for me to be trained as a doctor to serve my people. But it misfired, for a medical doctor was the one thing I didn't want to be. I didn't know what I wanted to be.

After the boat trip from East London to Cape Town, we were chauffeur-driven to a rambling country-style house at Claremont. The master of the house, umnini mzi, a sprightly old Boer wearing a white goatee and khaki shorts, introduced everyone to everyone. He told me and my little siblings to call him 'Oom Jannie', and to call a very fat smiling Boer lady 'Tante Beebas' and a small, very curly-headed lady 'Tant Isie'.

Oom Jannie took my hand and led me to an elderly couple

(elderly to my eyes, anyway; I was dismayed to see no children around) and said: 'And now, Nontando, here are your Uncle Arthur and Aunt Margaret who are taking you to England.'

I was surprised and thought: 'What, now? But we've only just come.' It was as if Oom Jannie had heard my thoughts because he said: 'But first, let's have tea. Then, Margaret, we'll all go and look again at our pride and joy.'

Jolly old man, he talked non-stop. This to me was natural. At home I was accustomed to the master of our house doing all the talking, cracking jokes, making his captive audience happy. It was the sort of South African household scene I knew.

Tante Beebas took me to sit on a sofa beside her and whispered as I gazed at my new Uncle Arthur and Aunt Margaret: 'You will like them very much, they are going to be nice to you, so don't worry – neh? And you won't be lonely, they've got children and young people, only they are out playing tennis with friends this afternoon,' and she warmly pressed my hand.

She was like the fat Boer ladies at home in our little town Alice, friends of my mother with whom she exchanged teatime visits and endless messages by hand of garden boys – to do with cookery recipes, pot plants and so on. They used to exchange copies of the *Farmer's Weekly* and a roneoed sheet of The Egg Circle; women with names such as Botha, Bezuidenhout, Petzer. Our town was a slow-flowing stream of non-racial friendliness and contacts between its resident Boers, English, natives – such names as Taylor, Glass, Burl, Tremeer, Jabavu, Bokwe and so on.

Tante Beebas murmured away and, like a well brought-up child, I kept quiet and listened. Which was just as well, for I was thinking that the one called Tant Isie was a coloured old lady. Again, to me quite in order, for we had coloured friends at home. Mr and Mrs Pease, for instance; their daughter was a great friend of mine.

Later I was to discover that my assessment of the curly-headed lady had been a childish thought indeed, nitwitted, for she was but Oom Jannie's pure Boer wife...But children can entertain the most unpredictable ideas!

When we all rose at Oom Jannie's bidding to follow him down his garden paths, he lifted my brother on to his shoulders, clasping the little ankles with one hand. And he and Aunt Margaret led the leisurely procession pointing at specimens – the 'pride and joys' – among the profusion of shrubs and creeping plants as they went with a walking stick and a folded parasol, talking animatedly.

Uncle Arthur, my mother and sister followed, she lifting up her arms to hold both their hands and prattling away unselfconsciously, grown-ups listening with amused attention.

Tante Beebas and I brought up the rear, I adjusting my step to hers, slow and stately because of her immense size.

It can't have been prior arrangement that Tante Beebas explained my new relations to me. Looking back, I imagine she was behaving naturally. Natives used to say that 'Boers are like us, are people, have humanity – linobuntu iBhulu. They like to communicate, as we do. A Boer can be your father, mother, and beat you, train you (ukuqeqesha) if you disobey his paternal commands. Don't we beat children, qeqesha them? Spare the rod and spoil the child. And the Boer can be so kind – oh don't talk about it! Unlike amaNgesi. They have not the warmth of the Boer. So 'correct' speaking through those closed lips and teeth, leave the black man to flounder by treating him as a mature creature with brains, stupid as we are – sizizidenge kangaka! No man, the Boer is better, is understandable. You know where you are with a Boer.'

Younger generations of my fellow blacks will be incensed to hear that such opinions were current, but it is fact. That is the kind of 'identity' the Boers had for some time before they developed the 'Afrikaner identity' of Dominee Vorster.

So, in 1933 Tante Beebas was behaving like 'a proper Boer' old lady, treating me as my mother would, had she not been busy discussing things with my new uncle. Black and Boer society in those days had, sociologically speaking, mores that were not dissimilar.

As her explanations drew to a close (for the party was now ambling back to the verandah), a chauffeur-driven limousine was waiting to bear us Jabavus to Newlands, where we stayed until my family sailed back to East London, leaving me suddenly disconsolate. Tante Beebas said comfortingly that she and the Oubaas were coming to England that summer – in a few weeks – and she'd come and see me again. 'And I'll find you happy like I've told you, promise?'

In England the following month sprightly Oom Jannie appeared on the scene. It was during the 'hols'. His arrival coincided with my fourteenth birthday, and I was bombarded with gaily wrapped presents from each member of my families – at home in England.

We had gone to our country cottage in Berkshire, botanising, birdwatching. At the cottage – at Aston Upthorpe – the idea was that we 'roughed' it as a health-giving change from Chippendale settees, mahogany dining tables. We went in two cars accompanied by our uniformed servants. They were put up comfortably in the village pubs. All of us slept in sleeping bags on the brick-flagged entrance hall which became a dormitory. Oom Jannie, next to him me, then Aunt Margaret, my 'sister' Helen, brother Nicholas, Uncle Arthur, and brother Anthony.

Next morning when Oom Jannie espied the birthday present-giving, he dashed upstairs to the room that was his rough workroom (he was making political speeches in Europe on this visit) and dashed down bearing a gift for me. He dropped on his haunches, beckoned me to him holding a little book, opened the flyleaf and inscribed: 'For dear Nontando on her 14th birthday J.C. Smuts.'

Then he smilingly teased me in guttural pronunciation: 'I've had no chance to wrap it up prroperrly, Nontando. How was I to know? You ladies are altogether too rreticent, secrretive about your passing yearrs!' and patted my head.

The slim volume was of course way beyond my understanding at the time. Many years later when I was able to read it, I was amazed. Oom Jannie's present was a copy of a speech he had delivered at St Andrews University, its theme 'Freedom'. And in it he developed a theory that freedom was not for the uncivilised black people of South Africa.

I couldn't help thinking: 'Old politicians are capable of unpredictable actions!'

Now it's my turn to put a question which suggested itself on reading Dominee Vorster's speech to the effect that liberals are more hateful, worse than communists, despoilers of the Afrikaner identity.

What would the Reverend Christian gentleman make of this small slice of non-racial South African behaviour abroad?

7

Going native in Mexico

꩜

16 FEBRUARY 1977

When in Rome, do as the Romans do . . .

If you are a woman and a black one and observe how locals dress, you try to do as they do for there must be a reason why their clothing has developed in the way it has.

Yet there are some aspects of Transkeian and Ciskeian women's fashions which I cannot bring myself to copy so far.

For instance, the wearing of bedroom slippers in the street, even in the mud! Is there a doctor who could explain the reason for this?

Or who could explain why Southern African 'European' children and young people are allowed by their parents to walk barefoot in streets, at any rate in Umtata, despite possible injury from broken bottles, pieces of glass, let alone tetanus?

I do understand why black men and women in Umtata carry or wear travelling rugs wrapped round their waists or draped from shoulders. It's because the geography of the region and its terrain is such that in winter it can get very cold indeed. And even in summer, the temperature during the day can change hour by hour from extreme cold to extreme heat.

So, although I've not yet brought myself to wear a rug over my trouser suit, I do wear the old-fashioned 'spencer' under my blouses. I also wear a typically South African garment called a 'body blouse'. Curious name; what's a garment for if it is not for the body?

It strikes me too that the black people's rugs (and pagan ladies' multiple number of petticoats and shawls) are lineal descendants of their animal skin karosses of pre-European days, which were protection from the violent extremes of temperature.

But I've not seen any South African whites dress as the blacks do. They've been in this country for something like 300 years, yet have their bodies adapted or not adapted to our climate, I wonder? Is the white body less susceptible to cold or heat? Or is it that they don't wish to look like 'natives'? Yet are they not native-born as we are? Or is it a cultural inheritance? Can a physician, or anthropologist or sociologist throw any light on the matter?

In the various countries I have lived in, the only one where I went native, so to speak, and wore the local peasant women's dress, was in Mexico. In the West Indies – especially in Jamaica and Trinidad – everybody wore any old thing. If you were comfortable in a pair of pyjamas, or Bermuda shorts or whatever, that's what you wore and nobody looked twice. In Mombasa it's like that too.

In Nairobi, some toffee-nosed Member of Parliament wanted to pass a law forbidding the wearing of miniskirts. My father's former Fort Hare student, the Attorney-General, Mr Charles Njonjo, replied – and he has a sense of humour – to the effect that if the Hon Member didn't like seeing legs, he could look the other way when such legs approached him!

In Malawi, wigs are forbidden by presidential decree. Also in Uganda. How about that? Yet wigs were invented in Africa, I believe. They are not a 'decadent European imported habit . . .'

Some years ago, when I went to live in Mexico for a time (when you have an independent income and no dependants, you can roam around wherever you wish!), I rented a hacienda a few miles out of Oaxaca. A hacienda (Spanish word) is a country farm type of house. I went there for peace and quiet after the bright lights of Kingston and Montego Bay to write – to increase my income. South Africans are deeply interested in how much money you've got!

I was surrounded by simple peasants. Gentle people who till the land, are agriculturists mainly, growing maize and sorghum.

A hacienda is a country house, a sort of farmhouse. Roomy, usually with high ceilings to the rooms; furnished sparsely. The drawing rooms are several. They face in different directions because the climate demands it. Cross winds, changing directions of light, just as here in Southern Africa. So, you need to control the capricious draughts, capricious behaviour of light. For this, you need louvred doors or windows, verandahs. Underfoot you need tiles. Some of the finest architects in the world are Mexicans.

The people who surrounded me, peasants, suggested I might try wearing their peasant dress. Very cheap, airy, wide at the hips in order to circulate the air round the body.

I took their advice.

My servant would come at around lunchtime to remind me that luncheon was ready in the dining room. She never really got used to my working all the time at writing. Peasants don't read. She would lead me to the dining room. I lunched alone of course, still thinking about words, sentences and grammatical constructions. She waited outside the door while the butler and footman attended to my needs.

Then when they signalled her in native language to come and take their lady to her room for 'siesta', she came and led me. She would pull out a stretcher from somewhere, and after arranging my clothing, she would put me to bed and herself lie on the stretcher near me. She was my chaperone!

In countries which have climates of the type in Mexico, South Africa, the Mediterranean, Mozambique and so on, is not this 'siesta' custom necessary, desirable?

I wonder why it is not observed in SA and Transkei? . . . Could an anthropologist or physician explain?

At around 7 pm my maid would arrange my evening clothes for socialising. Dinner. Guests. And would bring my Corgi bitch to accompany us. Her name was 'Zeegums' and she liked to lie at my feet under the dining table.

We talked, socialised, drank our tequila. Then maybe started eating at around 9 or 10 pm. At about midnight, my butler and foot-man would lead my guests to their Land Rovers and Jeeps. On other evenings, I myself was a guest somewhere, and my chauffer would drive me there.

Here in Transkei there is no such socialising. No dinner parties. What a boring town . . .

In the Republic of South Africa, social life between different races is forbidden by racialistic laws. Therefore, life in South Africa is too dreary for words. My white friends could not obtain permits to come to the Bantustan location in which I was staying, and I could not get a permit to go to their houses in the 'white' area of town where they lived.

What a country, what a government! Such cruelty over the space of a generation, which is how long I have been away from this land of my birth . . . It makes you sad.

8

All you need is love

උන්

23 FEBRUARY 1977

I have to write a letter instead of an article – an attempt to answer all the letters, telegrams and invitations you have written to me.

I am amazed, overwhelmed by your response to my voice crying in this wilderness of our lovely country in which, alas, we are restricted and forbidden to make friends across racial barriers.

On coming back here, all I expected was friendship, love, affection, communication.

I thought I was prevented. As indeed I am, we all are from communicating and loving one another – even talking to each other. By a ruling political party.

Politics interferes with our private lives. Yet, just through the medium of these articles, I find that other human beings – scores, hundreds – long to make friends across the colour barrier.

I've been sifting the letters that have arrived. Ninety-nine per cent say to me: 'Miss Jabavu – you love life! How wonderful to speak of it – tell me more!'

My Xhosa-speaking readers say: 'Yuh! Awunantloni Nontando, ukukhupha yonk' into?' ('Goodness! Are you not ashamed, disgusted at yourself, Nontando, to reveal everything like this?')

All races and ethnic groups long to communicate, to exchange views, especially about love, and loving one another, the most natural emotion.

Sifting these communications, I have found that the most

60

poignant need is love and that at present, my fellow blacks are ashamed of love and sex – but want to know about it!

Mna, andinantloni – me, I'm not ashamed, why should I be, and why should you be ashamed? What's wrong with love and affection?

We all need and hope for love, communication, affection, love. But I don't understand why you feel ashamed and disgusted. You feel ashamed yet are asking me to tell you more about my love life.

Well. I don't mind telling you.

I'm pushing 58 years, so naturally 40 at least have been full of love, children, family, career, widowhood, flirtations, warmth, love, affection, laughter. It's a full life. Music, reading, writing, love, love, love . . .

My fellow blacks ask: 'What's this being in love with a white man, a bachelor in Kenya? Many men here want your hand in marriage, ntombi kaJili, so why don't you marry one of our own black men and stay here?'

My answer to these scores of letters is that my own ideas about love (and my Kenyan white bachelor man friend agrees with me) is something like this: love is not for one to be a slave to the other. Black women here in South Africa are slaves, drudges.

My man friend in Kenya and I agree that freedom, democracy in the home, is what we, he and I, need. I'm a writer. He is a rich businessman only 39 years old. All my husbands and lovers have been younger than me. I don't know why.

Only 39, but so 'understanding'. And bossy, a real bully. We live in separate houses in Nairobi.

I don't like to drive my car myself nowadays. So, because of his affection for me, he orders his chauffeur to come to my house to pick me up in his Rolls Royce for my shopping. And to take me afterwards to his own house.

I arrive and am ordered: 'Lie down! I am doing the cooking today,' he says.

So, I obey. What else? He is over 1,9 m, I am under 1,6 m. So, I have to do what I'm told. Before he goes off to the kitchen to cook (with our houseboy), he brings me my bedside radio, switches on my favourite programme, and orders me: 'Sleep, dream; but don't get up. I'll come for you. Be good, do what I say!'

You see? He is a real Boer. And that's what I love about him. The whole relationship is a complex one. He and I don't sleep together.

When I was in Umtata gathering material for my book about my father, DDT Jabavu, I hoped for affection, warmth, kindness, from my fellow blacks.

Did I get it from them? No!

From whom did I get friendship?

From Boers – those tall, brown- or blue-eyed Boers of the Republic of South Africa seconded to Transkei Government, to help my Xhosa and Tembu people.

But I don't sleep with them.

Letters ask me: 'Who are you sleeping with?'

My answer is: 'That is hardly your business, is it? I myself know who I'm sleeping with, and you yourselves know what you are doing.'

I am happy to tell you everything, ukukhupha yonke into! And have I not indeed revealed quite a lot? And is it not now your turn, readers, to tell me something?

MARCH

'Chauvinism is bad in every way, but is so ingrained that it can take time, intelligence and much analysis to get rid of it.' This is the self-reflective Noni, in the third column of March. She is aware of her deep-seated biases and open to writing about them. In these five columns she writes about a theme that has been relevant to the South African psyche from time immemorial: class.

In the first, fourth and fifth columns, Noni discusses class in an overt way while in the other two columns, which have different concerns, class forms the backdrop in the writing.

In the first column 'Why I'm not marrying', she argues that being of the same social class as her husband(s) and/or partner(s) made for a better and more successful relationship. Today, discussions about the efficacy of hypergamy have been ignited in younger feminist circles. She also shares her reason for choosing not to marry again. In 'Why don't our Blacks read?', she writes '. . . to my chagrin, I now find that "my" so-called educated middle-class Xhosa home-people also don't read'. The fifth column, 'Friends in high places', opens with the death in February of Anthony Crosland, Britain's Foreign Minister at the time, and segues into nostalgia for her childhood in Oxford under the foster care of her in loco white parents who were and socialised with 'English tycoons, upper-class bankers, industrialists, conservative liberals'.

In the columns 'Could you eat her?' and 'Xhosa men have changed' class is implied. In 'Could you eat her?' she writes: 'The stevedores glance up and admire us lazy, rich people and make remarks.' Later in the column she mentions flats she owned in foreign countries. This column is also a commentary on the male gaze in public spaces and the lack of an 'own' culture among South African Europeans. The column about Xhosa men is a commentary on how men present in the public: 'I beheld . . . figures of a portliness, an obesity, a grossness that I hadn't remembered.' In this column Noni subtly connects men's presentation to class and upward mobility.

MAKHOSAZANA XABA

Above: Noni, walking
the streets of London
at age 28, 1947.
(Amazwi Museum Collection)

Below: Noni in a studio photograph,
22 March 1948 taken by Mme.
Yvonne, A.R.P.S., 98, Charing Cross
Road, London.
(Amazwi Museum Collection)

Above: Noni on Regent Street in London, August 1949.
(Amazwi Museum Collection)

Right: Noni standing on The Strand in London in 1961.
(Gallo Images)

Above: Noni, as editor of the magazine *New Strand* at her London office, 12th September 1961.
(Gallo Images)

Right: In her 28 September column, 'On peasants and possessions . . .', Noni has a lot to say about the décor and style of monied Black people in Uganda and South Africa, describing the living spaces as 'chockful' of 'awkward possessions'. This is her own home in Kingston, Jamaica, captured in 1963.
(Amazwi Museum Collection)

Noni and her friends Pat and Margot in May 1966 at Hope Road in Kingston Jamaica. *(Amazwi Museum Collection)*

9
Why I'm not marrying

🍵

2 MARCH 1977

From my observations since coming south last year, the emotion of 'love' differs among blacks and whites. You see how apartheid affects one's observations? In Kenya we don't think in these terms – we feel free to think and act naturally. But here I've had to adjust my bifocals.

When I first left my mother country at thirteen years, I was too young (and not precocious – I was a late developer) to have speculated on the matter. Since I went away, I've loved and been loved like anybody else.

And through circumstances beyond my control and the environments I was exposed to, my husbands or lovers were of widely different cultures, countries, creeds. My involvements with them succeeded when the gentlemen concerned were of the same social class as myself – my environment having been English ('Ingesi of the water' as we say in Xhosa), there was understanding between me and upper-class Englishmen. When I became involved with a black, it was disastrous, not because of colour, but class habits.

On coming back to live in Africa, so naive was I that I imagined all blacks were upper class like my father, from whom I inherited an atavistic love of black people. From that mistake, I was rescued by a fellow English upper-class gentleman, for his background in Kenya – an English aristocrat settler – gave him far greater knowledge of the mentality of 'my' fellow blacks. With few exceptions, black men regard a wife as a drudge, a child bearer for whom he has paid cattle (in East Africa they pay cows – imagine!).

Here in Southern Africa, on top of the Calvinist background, people are restricted and regulated by Government policy as to whom they may love, cohabit with, enjoy themselves with. An authoritarian policy which has arrogantly taken upon itself the power to kick down your bedroom door at night to check what colour body is embracing and loving which colour body!

Pursuing this thought, I'm now even wondering: are such masterpieces of art on the theme of love forbidden and banned here nowadays? Rodin, Epstein statues for instance?

Since many letters ask me in friendship rather than enmity to tell you more about my personal love life, I respond. Nothing in it to hide.

My love life goes on in its proper place, in Kenya, where it isn't forbidden as it would be down here, where my man friend and I would be 'put in' regardless of the fact that we are of the same English social class, and therefore share numberless class habits and assumptions, interests, friends. From habits in reading books down to habits in furnishing our abodes and food there's understanding, no friction.

'But being a widow and a bachelor, why don't you marry?' I am asked.

I've been married enough times, and unlike most blacks, I no longer imagine that bliss comes encircled in the wedding ring. And his attitude is that at his age, 40, and having experimented as any man does with transitory, trial girlfriends, he is satisfied in his voluntary commitment with this widow aged 58.

We agree about our separate need for privacy at times, for I have my writing to do and he has his vast business to attend to. He also likes hunting, safaris, mountain-climbing, bricklaying which I don't; and his bridge-playing!

Sometimes he cooks, sometimes I'm the one who cooks when we throw dinner parties.

Then there's the question of organising our money. This I regard as a man's job for I'm incapable of looking after mine.

He speaks perfect Swahili, having lived most of his life in Africa, whereas I've lived only less than half of mine in Africa. Therefore, he knows the black mentality and male attitudes better than I do – the peasant, lower-class greed, covetousness, rapacity, mendacity, deviousness. He had to protect me from being robbed right, left and centre, for in my naive atavistic idea that I am an African and am among my people, he had to open my eyes.

If he were a South African, you'd mistake him for an Afrikaner for he is tall, rangy, keeps his promises, is utterly reliable. My best friends here down south the year or more I've been here, like a Mrs Rip Van Winkle, are Afrikaners, formerly called Boers, in Kenya called affectionately in Swahili 'Kaburu'.

So, what do I need further in marriage? Isn't there enough trust, affection, loving care in my present relationship? Why tempt fate by altering it with signed contracts? Are we not grownups, mature?

According to him, though, I have a 'naughty' type of personality, am demonstrative. He says: 'Most black men are very vain. They don't understand your Europeanised kind of theatrical behaviour; your smiling, talking, holding their hands. They think it's an invitation to sex, not understanding that you are a writer, and have instinctive ways of drawing people out in conversation or over drinks.

'So', he added, on permitting me to come down south for a specific purpose, 'be good, no flirting, no confusing those black southern natives. Just write your book on your father and come back.'

Such, then, is my love life. I'm doing what I'm told.

10

Could you eat her?

༄

9 MARCH 1977

Last year on arriving by boat in Durban, something that usually happens to me when I sail into a new country happened again.

When the stevedores board the ship to handle the cargo, passengers are usually sitting on the sundeck watching men at work as they sip tea or Camparis, beers or milkshakes.

The stevedores glance up and admire us lazy, rich people and make remarks. If you understand the language, be it Greek, Italian, Swahili, Spanish, English, Xhosa or Zulu, you can crack up laughing.

In Durban docks, the stevedores were Zulu speakers of course. I am not a Zulu speaker although Xhosa is a related language, just as Afrikaans is related to German slightly and to Netherlands Dutch, so closely related that you can be quite confused.

These Zulu-speaking stevedores made jokes about me among themselves which I could understand:

'Couldn't you just eat that black lady?'

'Eat her? How could you? Where would you get the rands? Isn't she covered in golden finger rings and necklaces? That one would cost you more than a year's wages, man! Stop talking nonsense!'

'Do you think I wouldn't give up a year's wages to eat that one?'

They fell about laughing the way Africans can laugh, which is most infectious. I translated to my fellow passengers, and we in turn fell about laughing!

The dockworkers were behaving as dockworkers do all over the world, perhaps like men all over the world: men cannot help admiring women, I suppose.

Then we went ashore and were led into a sightseeing bus. The driver spoke to us on his loudspeaker and told us: 'Durban is for all European residents in Africa what the Riviera or other celebrated resorts are for us on the old Continent.' (He was forgetting me, black, with my flat in Geneva, my flat in Genoa and Antibes. Of course, I don't live in them anymore. I had to give them to my foster children for tax reasons. My man in Kenya, that vanilla gorilla of mine, told me to.)

We were driven on, and the driver talked what seemed to me a load of rubbish:

'This is the industrial area. See these black people?' We twisted our necks to see. 'They are blerry fond of drink. For tea break, they drink their Jabulani. Look at them.' We looked. 'It is hygienically made by the Government. We Europeans don't touch the stuff. It's for blacks only.' We gaped.

Next, we were taken to a house, and invited to walk into the garden. There we were invited to gaze upon what to me were absolutely hideous statues and statuettes of black women with babies on their backs, and black men carrying spears and knobkerries.

Next, we were taken to the Valley of a Thousand Hills and invited to gaze upon more blacks, naked . . .

Then we were driven back to our boat, to think things over. What I thought was something like this:

'South African "Europeans" seem to have no culture of their own. All that they seem to be mesmerised by is the culture of the blacks. What's wrong with them?'

11
Xhosa men have changed

ॐ

16 MARCH 1977

Whenever I moved to a country with a black majority – Uganda, Jamaica, Trinidad, Kenya – I used to start by declaring disdainfully: 'These natives are not handsome like my Xhosa blacks'.

Unjustly, of course. One becomes strangely chauvinistic and superior when abroad.

An atavistic emotion, and illogical as are all emotions. Just how illogical I didn't realise until I arrived in my mother country last year after an absence of two generations, during which my heart's memory had been filled with the beauty of my own Xhosa people.

I got a shock, was chagrined. For many weeks in Natal, Transkei, Ciskei where I was gathering material about my father, I had to wrestle with traumatic emotions on seeing that my people had become considerably less than beautiful, less than handsome.

Seated on my hotel balcony in Umtata, gazing at the Xhosa throng milling on the pavement below, I beheld a sea of elderly shaven, scraped heads gleaming in the relentless sun and figures of a portliness, an obesity, a grossness that I hadn't remembered.

These men were my own age group, pushing 60 years. I concentrated on them, iintanga zam. Their ugliness made me gasp. I was disappointed, deflated.

When I experience an emotional shock, I try to analyse the reasons for my reactions. I did so now, and gradually realised that having left Southern Africa at an impressionable age (thirteen years) my recollection of handsome Xhosa men had been influenced by the physique and personalities of members of my immediate family.

The handsomest of all had been my father, Prof DDT Jabavu, a man of exceptional good looks.

This is not just filial loyalty or pride. It was confirmed spontaneously, voluntarily, by everyone I met who had known my father.

Hearing that I was in Transkei to write a book about him, they referred to his beauty and urged me not to omit that aspect of his personality. A touching anecdote was told to me by a retired minister who said: 'Nontando, people were simple in those days. So, when other Africans subsequently followed your father in achieving BA degrees, they asked: 'Have these young men truly gained BA degrees, ugly as they are? A man must be inzwana, handsome, beautiful like DDTJ to be a BA...'

It's not the fault of my Xhosa age mates that their beauty falls short in my eyes. My memories had been made in another era. Forty years, 25 years ago, I don't remember seeing an educated, middle-class, prosperous African gentleman looking so fat as nowadays, and with his scalp scraped clean, shaven.

Kwowu ntanga zam, age mates of mine, you have disappointed me. Nindidanisile.

Because by comparison with developing countries in Africa, you South African blacks are highly developed. You drive huge cars, you dress in suits and collars and ties. You've obviously got money – more than my father or my uncles had. More than I myself have.

What is wrong with you? What are you trying to prove by making yourselves look so ugly with your scraped and shaven heads?

12

Why don't our blacks read?

≈

23 MARCH 1977

Some Wednesdays ago, in an article about me in a country district outside the small Mexican town of Oaxaca of about the size of Alice, or Umtata, I mentioned the puzzlement of my gentle Mexican house servants that I 'worked all the time – at writing books'. And I mentioned that my impression was that peasants don't read; therefore, I ascribed their surprise to the fact that through no fault of their own, they were analphabetics.

Because I was younger then and not using my brain properly to analyse our differing situations, I gave way to a chauvinistic and mindless opinion that these natives (who couldn't even speak Spanish or English) were vastly inferior to my own Xhosa in my mother country.

Alas, on coming back after many years to my South Africa, I've had to revise my opinion. And to try to expunge romantic chauvinism out of my system. Chauvinism is bad in every way, but is so ingrained that it can take time, intelligence, much thought, and self-analysis to get rid of it.

I've revised my opinion about peasants being the lower classes who don't read books, because to my chagrin I now find that 'my' so-called educated middle-class Xhosa home-people also do not read books.

During my year down here in Southern Africa, I've found that once a man or woman has swotted (it used to be called stalk-boring) at the required textbooks sufficiently to attain a diploma, certificate, or degree, that is the end of it.

In every household I've visited during my year here, the few books in sight gather dust behind locked glass cupboard doors.

My instinctive glance at the titles on their spines showed that they were textbooks. Maybe half a dozen volumes on such subjects as obstetrics, agriculture, education, mercantile law; occasionally a novel, *Mhudi*, or the play *Ityala lamaWele*; an occasional grammar book of some vernacular, or of English.

I'm talking about my fellow blacks. As one of you, you'll forgive me for expressing my impressions; these are not necessarily criticism, or disdain, but mere observation.

Chargrined as usual, I tried to analyse the source of my reaction. Finally, I realised that I'd been familiar with the presence of books in constant use – not dust-covered – in my parental home, kwaJili noMaGambu. Before they sent me overseas at thirteen years, I had rarely visited other households except on the Fort Hare campus.

During my decades away from South Africa, I had assumed in my romantic nostalgia that Xhosa homes were like ours at Fort Hare, kwa Nokoleji, where book-reading and discussing was part of the air we young ones breathed because that was how my parents organised the household.

I now find, more than 40 years on, that I was mistaken. The Jabavu home was not the norm. Nowadays, I find that once a person is capped BA, BSc or whatever, he or she feels educated and that they know all that needs to be known.

I now notice that the main occupation is conversation, incoko, if you can call it that, in the regional vernacular language.

And indeed, conversation in Bantu languages is extremely beguiling because, as my father's friend and colleague Prof Lestrade said (and I quote from memory as my personal library is in Nairobi), 'the vocalic, inflexional, onomatopoeic structure of this great family of related languages is full of beautiful imageries'. He gave examples in his books as a specialist in Suthu languages.

Apart from the reading matter always available at my home, conversation when my uncles came on visits or with my father's colleagues was of a type with meat in it as we say in Xhosa, meaning elevated, amusing, inokutya okuhluthisayo, containing nourishment for the brain.

It was wide-ranging, mind-stimulating, witty. Apart from my uncles on both sides, such people visited from time to time as the national poet SEK Mqhayi, the composer B-ka-T Tyamzashe, who I now realise is the Brahms or Vaughan Williams of South Africa, Ntinde and Ndlambe dignitaries, professors, lecturers, teachers from Fort Hare or Rhodes or Cape Town, Lovedale, Healdtown, overseas academics.

We young ones naturally kept quiet according to custom as we helped the housemaids serve trays of tea to our elders and their guests, but our ears were flapping, hearing, conveying messages to our formative brains. I carried such scenes away with me as being the normal South African household life.

What do I find now, more than 40 years on? No reading of books; conversation utterly desultory, puerile ... 'Ninjani? How is everyone here at Home?' 'Hayi, sikho. Ninjani nina? No, we are all right. How are yourselves?' 'Oh, ewe, sikho, sihamba nazo. Oh, yes, we are alive, we go along with our problems (these coughs and colds)' ... for minutes on end punctuated by stagnant silences, eyes avoiding other eyes and gazing at the mealie patch outside the front door.

Meaty, witty, general conversation as of old? If you are thinking in such terms – as I naively was on coming down south last year – you'll need to readjust your ideas, accept disappointment, yet try to analyse, understand, make allowances. My own circumstances have been different, and perhaps your own, through no fault of ours.

I am chagrined but trying to understand and analyse. And what I needed during this long visit to my own people was an explanation. Did I get it? Alas, no. Is this non-communication possibly because I speak too directly, like a 'European-of-the-Water'? If so, I can't help it. Kaloku abazali bam bandigibisela phesheya ndiselula, my parents 'threw' me overseas while I was still a light-weight child. So, I am not accustomed to this black people's beating about the bush, this devious conducting of non-conversations about health/impilo, drought, rainfall, any real 'meat for the brain' being studiously avoided. Or is it non-existent or too ghastly to contemplate?

On returning to Kenya ten years ago to live permanently, I knew people would read less there than we southern blacks had – as I'd imagined – 40 years ago because Western education had reached East Africa far later. No Lovedales there of over a century.

But I got two surprises now that Kenya is independent. The first was that the highly educated blacks are like ours down here of these days. They don't read. The degree is the thing, then books are put away to gather dust.

The second was that the 'lower classes', youths who've had a minimum of secondary education, are veritable stalk-borers of such cheap paperbacks as they can afford.

Outside the grocer's shop I frequent on the main street of Nairobi, a young Kikuyu in his early thirties runs a second-hand paperback business on the pavement. After getting to notice him, I sold him at a nominal price (for people are said not to appreciate free things) the paperbacks I've finished with. He resells them to passers-by of all races but mostly impecunious young black stalk-borers. With his profits, he maintains his young family.

From me he gets such paperbacks as Robert Graves' historical novels, others by Evelyn Waugh, Nevil Shute, Graham Greene, Gavin Lyall, VS Naipaul, the Trinidad Indian – that prince among writers.

This enterprising young man is only one among hundreds in Nairobi and other towns plying this trade. In between making sales, he sits on his upturned orange box and reads the books to himself, laboriously using his lips. I often sit beside him and we chat. I find that he is becoming discerning. The questions he asks me show this. He realises that these books are not only entertaining, but mind-improving (in Xhosa zizikutya, they are food for the brain).

Since I've been travelling down here for over a year now, and as usual acquiring paperbacks, I've looked for humble booksellers of his type. Do you think I've seen a single one? So, I post my used paperbacks to my pavement bookseller friend in Nairobi!

Meanwhile, I ask myself: what would our forefathers down here feel if they saw us now, having struggled, sacrificed, to educate us? Would they not turn in their graves?

13
Friends in high places

༜

The death of Anthony Crosland, Britain's Foreign Minister, saddened not only those who knew him well, but gave me food for thought on the subject of environment. Not pollution and all that. I mean: what is it that influences a person's upbringing?

I met Tony Crosland before World War II. He was at university, I was still at school. During the holidays, I was among the young ones who were imperiously summoned by our clever elder 'brothers' to their student political offices to do menial work such as addressing envelopes, making tea, or to paint placards declaring 'Down with this or that!'

Tony Crosland was one of these bossy ones, of whom we younger ones were in awe, and we obeyed his commands.

How did I get mixed up in all this in my teens?

Because the family I lived with in England were English tycoons, upper class, bankers, industrialists, conservative liberals. Their children were at the most expensive English public schools. I was put into one such school.

My 'brothers'' friends were the late Tony Crosland, the late Mohan Kumaramangalam, the late Ram Nahum, the late Feroze Gandhi whose widow is Mrs Gandhi, former Prime Minister of India, and daughter of the late Jawaharlal Nehru and niece of Mrs Pandit.

I was such a slow developer I had no idea that Tony Crosland was only my age when he used to breeze into the office wearing his belted camel-hair coat and order us about. His own political organisation was the University Labour Federation (ULF).

I was only vaguely aware that our elders were distressed by the politicking, rebellious behaviour of their young. For instance, my English family 'brothers' picketed outside Morris Cowley Works on the side of the workmen.

Their father, my Uncle Arthur, a banker, was furious, for he had advanced funds to William Morris (later Lord Nuffield) to change from manufacturing bicycles to motor cars at Cowley, near Oxford. My Uncle Arthur maintained several family cars, two of them Morris Cowleys which we called the little cars; the others were Daimlers, maroon colour, the same type saloons as King George V and Queen Mary used.

A family row broke out one morning when my Uncle Arthur told his sons (my brothers): 'You can jolly well WALK to Bill Morris's Cowley Works with your placards. I forbid you to use my cars. Rebels don't drive cars!'

The row of course was in gentle English upper-class tones of voice, and no beating or fighting. So, being young, I didn't really know what was going on! And apart from my youth, I kept getting bouts of homesickness for South Africa, my mother country, because Cato Smuts Clark always reminded me of home; daughter of my Oom Jannie, married to one of my cousins, Bancroft Clark, of the shoe manufacturing family.

When the maroon Daimler saloon was exchanged for a new Armstrong Siddeley Saloon one morning, my Uncle Arthur held my hand to look at it as it was being delivered, and recited a line from a Shelley poem, 'Ozymandias of Egypt'. Armstrong Siddeley cars in those days had a little sphinx on the bonnet.

All these things were way above my woolly little head at the time!

All the deaths of my age mates, the latest Tony Crosland's, make me wonder why am I still alive and feeling like a spring chicken. And this so-called environment. How come that surrounded as I was in my teens in England by millionaire bankers, industrialists and so on, I know nothing about how to manage my money, and politics is a closed book to me?

Yet I became a wife, mother, grandmother, writer. I seem to have inherited what scientists call genes. Those of my father and mother. Professor and Mrs DDT Jabavu crossed and produced me and my sister, and late younger and only brother.

The influences of later contacts in my youth in England didn't overcome the influence of my parents. The awful homesickness I suffered from, despite being in the best surroundings anyone can imagine . . .

All I think I can say to Tony Crosland, Mohan Kumaramanga-lam, Feroze Gandhi, is 'Farewell; Ndlelantle, isitya esihle asityeli' (a difficult phrase to translate into English but it means something like: 'a beautifully made dish for eating out of is not used for eating, but is kept to be admired and respected for its memories').

More than 40 years on, my return to South Africa for my protracted visit has opened my eyes to many things. So, farewell, Tony Crosland! You were one of these 'beautiful dishes'!

APRIL

～

'The Ochre People of Transkei' echoes back to Noni's book *The Ochre People* (1963) as she describes the traditional Xhosa people she encounters while travelling Mthatha. Noni refers to the ochre people as pagans, which intimates the Xhosa word iqaba referring to Xhosa people who rejected Christianity and Western education. Beneath this description lies a nostalgia for the binary created between amaqaba and amagqobhoka – the unconverted and the converted – created in the book she references, *Xhosa in Town – Townsmen or Tribesmen* by P Mayer. While she is a part of the African elite who are often seen to eschew anything related to their Xhosa heritage, her use of language and appreciation for isiXhosa as a complex language is explored in the column 'Just use your ears'. The tinge of nostalgia continues in this column as she tells stories about her love for language and how it influences her writing. It seems she is a writer who pays attention to the world around her, despite the time she has spent away from home.

The thread of travel which emerges from her books as well as her editorials finds itself in April. However, this is not simply a reflection about how 'Travel only confuses the mind' but also a commentary about the political nature of travel, as she is aware that within the context of 'petty apartheid' her children and grandchildren cannot join her as she travels South Africa because of segregation.

The final column connects identity with travel as Noni explores the naming practices she has witnessed in her two homes, South Africa and England. This column captures Noni's status and identity construction as she openly admits 'In England where I – a South African black – lived for 40 years as an upper-class white (not my fault)...' and she continues to explain the relations she had with members of the upper class and royals. This admittance seems very nonchalant but part of the honesty which is so pervasive in her writing.

ATHAMBILE MASOLA

14
The ochre people of Transkei

6 APRIL 1977

The Ochre People is the title of one of my books: but I'm not advertising it here — I want to talk today about my own ochre people in their flesh. When I was in Transkei the spectacle of them in Umtata streets bowled me over.

I begin with the women (ladies first: black gentlemen won't like that of course). How beautifully they walk and carry their slim bodies! How their costume becomes them — that flowing shawl over the shoulder, that very feminine skirt which sways from side to side at the heels as the womanly hips twitch from side to side! The apotheosis of sexiness, this movement. How provocative!

Yet the lady is covered completely — from head to toe. Why, then, are such women more sexually arousing than their bikini-clad sisters of the world? Because their dress leaves everything to the male imagination. An unshapely, or indeed a shapely, one is less exciting in manly eyes if she exposes her whole body. He prefers to imagine, cogitate, on what might be underneath those clothes.

I was told this male attitude by my most favourite lover some years back and I did indeed believe that big blond bully of mine!

Staring at these breathtakingly beautiful female figures, starting from their feet, I noticed that when wearing shoes, they wore men's shoes. I wondered why, but realised that men's shoes are better designed to fit one's foot. Women's latter-day shoes are plain silly and can wreck the metatarsal bones. (Don't forget that in

England, one of the white families I was brought up by were shoe-makers, Clarks of Street, so I know!)

But just above the shoes (which are for town use, incidentally), I was surprised to see that Pondo pagan women wore many rings of coloured plastic thongs instead of the rings of brass wires of olden days. Hideous. But fortunately, almost hidden by the beautiful braided skirt . . .

I examine the pagan lady's turban, the 'Iqhiya enkulu', that stunning head-dress. Not only is it breathtakingly arranged – I gradually remembered that in fact it is a species of handbag!

Pagan ladies carry their money in it. You never see them carrying the usual type of handbag, the 'rubbish-heap, Anglo-Saxon midden,' that civilised women like me carry around. Pagan ladies organise themselves more efficiently. The turban, and the front apron – 'incibiba' – of a married woman are capacious, graceful pockets.

Then I studied their menfolk. My, how attractive! In my 'naughtiness', I admit I could fall for them. Such maleness, such authority, the atmosphere of responsibility they exude as they stride in front of their wife – yuh! How I wished (atavism again) I belonged to a Red Man!

These wishes and longings – the only way to deal with them is to analyse them. Try to use your little brain . . .

I tried to, with the help of one of my favourite books, called *Xhosa in Town – Townsmen or Tribesmen* by P Mayer, which I carry around wherever I go.

I noticed how the pagan menfolk dress nowadays when in town: starting from their tops, they wear a Stetson hat (usually brown) set squarely on the head. On an ear is often a double earring. Then an ordinary town suit and clean shirt. And of course, a pagan gentleman carries the inevitable knobkerrie, 'intonga' in our language.

And as for when a Xhosa pagan man rides into town on horseback, dressed as I've described, looking like a medieval knight, I used to almost swoon ('faint', kaloku mna nditheth' isiNgesi nina ningakhumshi ke!) watching them from the balcony of my hotel room in Umtata.

But I asked myself, why do I never see 'Christian, school people' talking to our beautiful ochre people?

So, I reread my Mayer book which I've carried round since 1962 to relearn, refeed myself about the differences that exist between townsmen and tribesmen.

A splendid book. But my fellow Southern blacks don't read books. Only textbooks: and when they've passed their degrees, that's the end of it – isn't it? 'Shame!' (as Southern Africans black, brown, white, like to exclaim. This is a word construction that I must one day analyse!)

If you want, or can bother yourself, to learn about atavistic feelings and your neuroses, fellow black people, please read Mayer's *Townsmen or Tribesmen*.

Intombi kaJili iyaningxolisa ngoku! – she is scolding you!

84

15
Just use your ears

ᴗ৶

13 APRIL 1977

Those of you who have read my books by begging, borrowing or stealing them (you think I don't know?) are writing to me: 'Miss Jabavu, how do you manage to write such true, natural sounding conversations? You are very clever. Please let me come to your room and learn from you privately how to do it' ...

Thank you for these complimentary remarks. Alas, however, I cannot answer you individually. So, I hope you'll accept the explanation which I'm about to give you jointly.

The way I write 'true, natural-sounding conversations' in Xhosa (which I don't do often because I am an English-language, not a Bantu-language writer) is like this: it's by using the ears!

Often, when seated on the verandah of my Umtata hotel, ready to write a paragraph of a book or article, my ears were assaulted, almost deafened, by conversations being conducted on the pavement below by Xhosa speakers who possess splendid voices that carry, as do those of Wagnerian opera singers.

So, I put aside my work to listen. And what interesting sentences of natural conversation I heard. I noted them down immediately.

Such remarks as 'Yuh!' (and here I must transliterate for the benefit of non-Xhosa speakers), 'Andaphoxeka, mntakwethu by that Government servant! What a fool he made of me, saying he was helping my case and all that, kwatsha kwacima ... ka-nti! (and yet!) all along exoka telling lies. Taking my money yet doing bugger-all for me. Why? Because of taking money from the other side, my opponents, telling them lies also and doing bugger-all for them either. Oh, we black people, we are deceivers by creation. Thixo!'

One day, walking in town with one of my first cousins, we overheard an overalled manual worker, iqaba, umntu' obomvu, a member of the class of Xhosa I've called the ochre people in one of my books. He was giving a resounding monologue to a group of interested fellow workers leaning on their picks and spades.

'Bafondini!' – again I must transliterate for the benefit of non-Xhosa speakers – 'Fellow men! From today you must purify your speech. That word which is spelt MNQUNDU wakho? Pas op, bafondini! It was used in Parliament by a whole chief, and they led the chief out of that nkundla (men's meeting place). We've got our nkululeko independence now, so we blacks must talk politely, even whole chiefs, let alone me and you!'

As he and his audience doubled up laughing, my cousin and I halted to spell out the word to each other. It was the anatomical 'rectum' but with a sarcastic connotation. It was my cousin and I who now cracked up laughing!

The ochre people used to be – and perhaps still are – totally un-abashed in their use of language. Therefore, as a child of 'school!' or 'educated' people 45 years ago, I was among those whose nurse-maids forbade us to mingle with ochre people's children.

Another time, crossing the bridge alone over the Umtata River, two young men behind me were discussing in resounding baritone voices their problem of being jobless. As they overtook me, greet-ing me 'Molo, sisi,' one shouted to the other (in Xhosa of course): 'Why don't we join the police, man?' The other, startled so that his baritone rose at least an octave, shouted back: 'What – me? How can I ever, mfondini, such a persistent breaker of the law as I am?

Mus' ukudlala ngam, mfo – don't play with me, man!' I couldn't help smiling – who could? – as I watched them giving each other energetic, friendly blows on shoulders and ribs and laughing their heads off.

That incident made my day, for didn't it contain the elements of a Tolstoy novel or Terence Rattigan play?

One morning, soon after Transkei gained independence and when people were collecting the identification photos they'd posed for, among the huge, pushing, shouting throng I overheard a man yelling as he glared at his picture: 'Thyini! (exclamation!), Thixo! (God!) So, I am as ugly as this?'

Someone asked equally loudly: 'Don't you have a mirror at home?'

Answer: 'Thank God I can't afford one – I'd have fainted dead years ago at the sight!' Everyone roared.

When you've long forgotten such things, you marvel at the capacity of black people's natures the world over, West Indies, USA, Kenya, even here, for joyfulness despite hardship. In one of his books, Gen Smuts (my Oom Jannie, remember?) speaking as a botanist observed that the African continent is so harsh an environment that God gave the black man this enormous capacity for joy and endurance . . .

This is how I write what you call my 'natural, true-sounding conversations'. It's not by being clever. I couldn't possibly invent such dialogues. All I do is use my ears as my parents taught me to from childhood. You don't need to have degrees as long as you have ears. Are they not God's gift?

16
Travel only confuses the mind

❦

20 APRIL 1977

Travel broadens the mind, people say. I wonder if they believe this or are 'just talking, bathetha nje', only to make empty conversational noises.

Travel, which has been my lot because of circumstances beyond my control, doesn't broaden mine much. It confuses it. The things I see, hear, or am told, make what passes for my mind into a sort of kaleidoscope.

Travelling is in fact very upsetting for a woman. Women like to be in their permanent nest. Making homes across continents can be a marriage-breaker. That's one of the reasons I've been married more than once – but not as often as Elizabeth Taylor!

When you travel, your mind gets into difficulties: the sights, the smells, the vegetation. All these make me wish I were a trained botanist, geologist, ear, nose and throat specialist, and that my memory was better.

For instance, you meet so many people. In lands where blacks are in the majority, I get confused about distinguishing individuals from others I've met somewhere, sometime.

Was it Noel Coward who said in a song about Chinese people: 'They all look alike to me'? Well, I now know what he meant, for although black myself, having lived in so many black lands 'all blacks look the same to me'.

Here in my mother country, when some black person greets me

in the street in Xhosa, I answer in English or Swahili, mistaking him or her for some West Indian or East African or Afro-American. Why? Because I've lived most of my adult life in Kenya and Uganda. So, my mind has to quickly reprogram its computer!

Xhosa speakers can be very amusing: a distant relative of mine on meeting me last year asked in a loud Xhosa voice, and here I must transliterate into English: 'Don't you remember me? I, who used to push you in your pram?' How could a 57-year-old answer such a question?

And when I was in Umtata, the trees round about reminded me of a species of tree I had admired in avenidas (avenues) of Mexico City, and when I was in Natal, the pines reminded me of pine trees I'd seen in Canada.

And the rock formations in Transkei, those outcrops (are they still called kopjies, I wonder) reminded me of the ones you see in Canada when you drive from Toronto to Calgary, Alberta, passing through little towns with quaint names like Medicine Hat.

And grapevines in Canada reminded me of grapevines in France or Spain.

And the money – oh goodness! What I do during my present pro-tracted visit to Southern Africa is to hand all my cash to my first cousin when we go shopping, because I don't understand the dif-ference between the coins of nowadays.

When I was a child, we spoke in terms of pounds, shillings, pence. And in Xhosa a half-crown was ihalfgolweni, and one and six was indaliso. Nowadays, when I say 'rands or rand' in my English accent (which I can't help), I am gaped at. Apparently, I should say 'runt'.

In Kenya, we speak of money in terms of shilling. When I visit my grandsons in London, I don't understand the new money. So, I hand my cash to my grandson. He knows all about the new metric money, the Pee. What a strange name in my elderly ears!

When I visit my foster grandchildren in Florida, USA, I hand my money to my granddaughter. If we fly to Bimini (Bahamas) to the cottage I gave her parents, she or they manage my cash. They under-stand the American dollar, and it seems to please all of my teenage grandchildren to help their 'grannie from Africa', as they call me.

When my daughter turned seventeen or eighteen, I took her to Spain to picture galleries, the Prado and so on. It confused my mind that she didn't enjoy the trip one bit. She, Thembi, was born in England in 1942, and is therefore by culture an Englishwoman. She hated being admired openly – '*muy guapa*' (Spanish for 'very pretty').

Being so utterly English, she didn't like men to admire her pret-tiness in the street, out loud. The custom she was accustomed to was that when an Englishman sees a pretty girl – and she is ex-ceedingly pretty – he looks the other way! Or did when she was a teenager. Maybe their behaviour has changed now that she is 35.

Well, as she hated being called very pretty by Spaniards, I took her to Italy. I couldn't have made a worse mistake.

'Mummy, they are pinching my bottom! I want to go home!' But I had work to do in Rome. So, I put her on a plane home to England. My own bottom was being pinched now and again in buses, but at my age I was mature enough to take no notice. I remained to do my writing.

My children and grandchildren would love to come to South Africa to see the memorial to my father DDT Jabavu and my aunt, Miss Cecilia Makiwane. But we'd all have a hard time because we are all different colours. Separate development would prevent us from being together overnight in one house.

Overseas, we and everybody read Mr Pik Botha's announcement at the United Nations that petty apartheid was being done away with in six months.

What did he mean?

17
The names people are given

27 APRIL 1977

When a child is about to be born to you if you are a middle-class white, a friend possibly gives you a 'Name for Baby' booklet.

In England where I – a South African black – lived for 40 years as an upper-class white (not my fault!), my betters, the aristocrats, and their own betters, the Royals, followed an hierarchical system of naming their babies. That system is not unlike that of the Kikuyu tribe in Kenya where I live now.

In England, the Royal Family use, for instance, Elizabeth, Alexandra, Mary, Margaret for their female babies, for their male babies George, Henry, Edward, Charles and so on. The Kikuyu tribe is also rigid in this respect: babies are named after alternate grandmothers and grandfathers on both sides – father and mother. So, you get very few and unimaginative names. Girls: Wailimu or Wanjiru; boys: Mwangi, Njuguna, and so on. East African blacks do, however, enjoy themselves in their choice of 'European' names for their progeny. Scholastica, pronounced Scholar Sticker; Emperor Vespasian, pronounced Empela Veraspas.

What I enjoyed on coming back to Southern Africa in 1976 was to note the poetic freedom in which my Xhosa tribe really let themselves go when naming their children in Xhosa names. They took these names for granted and didn't notice. Whereas to my own ears, having been away for so long and having had to use many languages, these names were breathtakingly dramatic, poetic, historic.

Let me show you what I mean. I'm compiling my own 'Name for Baby booklet' . . .

Gcinumzi: Custodian of the homestead – for a boy baby.

Usinde Phi: How did you escape? For a boy or girl baby.

Zenemvula: Came with the rain.

Ntombizanele: Enough girls.

Impayipheli: The army of baby boys is unending!

Thembelihle: Good Hope . . . the youngster so named whom I met was in fact a little rascal.

Notomato: Must have been a bumper tomato harvest when she was born.

Nogogogo: Was born in a shanty tin hut in an urban area. You have to contrive a house for yourself and family out of the available material, tin paraffin cans, amagogogo because of influx control, and so on . . .

Mlahleni: Throw-him-away. My imagination boggled at the volume of suffering contained in the family background of that naming.

As it indeed boggled again at another one I met, 'Waliwe' (You are rejected) . . .

I was also – and still am – thinking about a very popular name nowadays for boys and girls, which I had never heard of 40 years ago and whose source or derivation I cannot fathom. Pinkie, in native (black) pronunciation, 'Peeenkie' – the ugliest and blackest people I met were called Peeenkie! I am baffled.

Turning my brain to a different but pleasanter puzzle of nomenclature, many blacks I've met were called Joubert, Merwe (short for Van der Merwe), Graaf (short for De Villiers Graaff), young chaps in their twenties. To me, this was extraordinary!

The only white children with black names I know of are a small boy named Vuyani (Be Glad), and a small girl named Vuyelwa (difficult to render into English but meaning something like 'of gladness' – one of those reciprocal verbs).

My brain, sparked off on this visit, turned to the names of some of our Xhosa Royals, our princes, kings, paramount chiefs: Botha, Tudor, Kaiser ...

English speakers or Afrikaans speakers might think that Botha is in honour of some Afrikaner soldier. You'd be in error. I was, too, until my old-fashioned Xhosa language memory came back and I realised that 'Bota' – singular – or 'Botani' – plural – is a pure Xhosa verb for 'I greet you' – singular – or 'I greet ye'.

I am still puzzling over the derivation of the splendid Royal names Tudor (Ndamase, a Pondo prince) and Kaiser (Matanzima, a Tembu 'prince' or 'duke'). These Xhosa Royals are the grandest of feudalists. As a commoner, you have to abase yourself in their presence and never, ever, call them by their name.

In England, I could and do call feudal dukes or princes by their name George or John or Philip or whatever. But here? In Xhosa society? The nearest familiarity I may express is to hail 'Ah, Daliwonga; Ah, Dalin-dyebo; Ah, Tshawe; Ah, Ngonyama,' and in doing so must genuflect, and lower my eyes because no commoner may look at a royal in his eye! ...

MAY

ᔇᔈ

'Travel, while not necessarily broadening the mind, makes you less censorious.' From this quotation in the first column in May we read that being 'less censorious', like being less chauvinistic, are lessons that Noni has learned from life. These are lessons she also seems to have aimed to live by.

Noni starts her May columns with one she calls: 'Shebeens all around me' which, like the other columns, gestures away from the title-suggested theme to a broader one. These May columns return to the quintessentially Noni-esque theme of travel. On the first Wednesday, Noni compares the conduct of police officers in Jamaica, Kenya, Britain and South Africa, where she had travelled extensively.

In 'Keeping tabs on tots', her second column, Noni delves into the impact of apartheid laws on human behaviour, using the cocktail party she hosted as a holder for the conversation about how the apartheid regime keeps tabs on Black people's lives.

The travel theme continues with the phrase 'Unyawo alunampumulo', as Noni writes in her third column. This column is about travel in real and metaphorical ways. Using the isiXhosa expression, Noni writes about how travel often embeds surprises in it. Noni was moving between homelands and 'South African' soil as the apartheid policies directed. She writes: 'Grahamstown is where I now am. Associate fellow of Rhodes University Institute for the study of English in Africa and guest of University Institute of

Social and Economic Research in my capacity as researcher of documents and materials for my projected biography of my father.'

Even when writing about relationships in her last column in May, she uses a travel metaphor: 'It takes time to find your way around the jungles of mating procedures.' In this quote, love relationships are a jungle deserving of skilful navigation and commitment to spending time.

MAKHOSAZANA XABA

95

18

Shebeens all around me

∽

4 MAY 1977

Shebeens to be made legal ... The day that headline hit my eyeballs, I nearly fell off my chair in surprise. Because all the time I'd been back in Southern Africa, it hadn't crossed my mind – or anyone else's to tell me – that the shebeens they showed me were illegal.

I assumed that the people I saw streaming into next-door houses which I was told matter-of-factly were shebeens, as were others around in the locations, towns, and 'ezilalini' – country villages – which I visited or stayed at in Natal, Transkei and Ciskei were simply going about their ordinary boozing business. They went about it determinedly, day and night. This didn't surprise me because many countries I've lived in don't follow the British style of 'opening and closing times' for pubs and bars.

What did raise one of my eyebrows, though, was to see uniformed policemen enter these shebeens in broad daylight to drink. In Kenya our police, having been trained by the British, are true-blue black bobbies. Wouldn't dream of breaking a law. So British bobby-like indeed that they really are 'your friend' as a member of the public. If in trouble or lost, you head for a policeman.

One of my best friends and protectors in Nairobi is a huge, pitch-black, champion heavyweight boxer, Kikuyu Inspector of Police. Imagine down here chumming up with a policeman! I'm told that here one's reflex on sighting an arm of the law is to take to one's heels.

In Jamaica the men in blue, trousers striped red down the side, are equally British. But, typically West Indian, they temper tradition. When patronising bars (despite being on duty) for that tot of 'The Two Waters' (that's rum and water – the local beer is even named after their uniform, Red Stripe), they respect the proprieties by removing their caps!

I've found so many things done differently in South Africa from anywhere else that again I didn't let myself dwell overlong on the spectacle of the southern men in khaki 'doing their thing' along with everyone else. Travel, while not necessarily broadening the mind, makes you less censorious . . .

But what did dwell on my mind was the shock of discovering, in my own home village Middledrift, which I'd remembered as so innocent, that within veritable spitting distance of my father's house every other house, round or square, was a shebeen!

Middledrift had been a stronghold of the IOTT in my parents' day: the International Order of True Templars. 'I Only Take Tea', as the disrespectful used to call it. My late brother and his fellow students at Witwatersrand University even actually Took Only Hot Water and Milk, bless them . . .

I'd imagined Middledrift was as conservative as a small town can get. After all, wasn't it founded the same year as Johannesburg? And has it changed as Johannesburg has? No, indeed. Not a single skyscraper blots its splendid landscape.

But its progress can be gauged by the sophistication of its shebeens, for these even cater for the different classes of black society. I was shown those frequented by customers who dressed and conversed like the 'jakwa' roughneck types, and those by the travelling elite, Middledrift being on a main road; gentlemen from faraway places who dressed and conversed like teachers, doctors, magistrates.

'Khawufane ucinge', just think of it. I nearly fell off my chair listening to those details. Indeed, as the months passed I became, as it were, bruised all over from falling off chairs at the changes that have taken place during my Rip Van Winkle absences.

Next week: More on the Demon Drink.

19
Keeping tabs on tots

❧

11 MAY 1977

As far as I could remember about Africans and demon drink – the 'Destroyer', so named at home – blacks had been strictly prohibited from buying or consuming 'European' liquor. A small number of highly educated might qualify for a special permit.

Since coming here in 1976 I learned that in 1962 the Nationalist Government lifted all liquor restrictions applying to blacks and booze, in the teeth of bitter opposition from the then African National Congress who, knowing their own people better than the Government, feared that blacks would drink themselves blue in the face.

So, I asked in wonderment: 'Is that one of the reasons the ANC was banned – offering advice which the Government didn't want to hear?' I was answered with doleful head shakings: 'Noni, better leave this. Haven't you said yourself you are a political half-wit, that the moves and countermoves of politics are above your head?'

So, by way of answer I was taken to see for myself one or two of the drinking parlours – halls? dens? – that the Government's Bantu Administration Department has established over the years with the object of raising funds for Government-controlled Bantu development, and to have it explained to me why responsible Africans disapprove of money being raised in this way 'for their own good', especially by God-fearing, puritanical, presumably abstemious Calvinists.

One such establishment at the little country village of Qumbu is right beside a national road. I saw crowds of black men and women, mostly dishevelled and ragged, sitting or lying on the ground pouring drinks out of bucket-like, garish coloured, plastic containers, and young children lugging some of these home for their elders, staggering under the weight.

And around those squatting as they quaffed, or stretched out prostrate and dead to the world, were others teetering, weaving, swaying as we say 'beqhuba amatakane', driving goat kids. A typically arresting Xhosa image of the tottering gait of the inebriate.

Later that year the Soweto and Langa riots broke out. For passionately felt reasons of protest, militant youth attacked and smashed those Bantu Administration drinking palaces, also bottle stores, shebeens, declaring their elders were degrading and destroying themselves.

I sympathised with these young protestors although for simpler and lesser reasons. My own inward protest arose because the sight at Qumbu had been to my mind an ugly, humiliating spectacle, degrading, unaesthetic, an offence to the sensibilities. It broke one's heart to compare it with the spectacle I beheld when my cousin drove me to visit his parents' and our Makiwane grandparents' graves deep in the country.

We passed a gathering of 'ochre people, abantu ababomvu' enjoying a rural weekend alfresco drinking party, 'utywala nenyama, meat and drink'. Everyone was resplendent in red robes, their 'clothes of home' pagan dress. Some sat in a great circle on the green grass watching the dance, others in separate groups of men one side, women on another, young men there, young girls elsewhere.

All so decorous, dignified, yet jolly; a scene of controlled happiness, aesthetic to a 't'.

Living in hotels as I did here, I threw cocktail parties. Refusing to be browbeaten by the heavy mantle of Calvinistic guilt, I did as I naturally do in my own home – normal socialising, to meet people. And dash it all, hadn't I come south to feel again the texture and society of my mother country?

I enjoyed my guests and they seemed to enjoy coming despite my stipulating on the invitation: 'From 6:30 pm to 8:45 pm.' (Very unblack this – eh? Even at home in Nairobi it raises blacks' eyebrows.)

But I didn't mind even those who came uninvited, types who overstay to empty every bottle you put out. One has to pay for lessons – not so? And I wanted to learn more about those shebeen businesses: why folks patronised them despite gross overcharging, and how come they operated blatantly, yet were illegal?

There was an awkward pause. My guests that evening were two married couples in their thirties, earnest young teachers longing to be informal, yet shyly inhibited in deference to my age. They were accompanied by a bright 'uninvited' whose name I didn't catch.

They exchanged sideways looks when I asked. The young ladies blushed and cast their eyes down, their husbands silent. The uninvited declared: 'Oh, so many things, Auntie. The reasons responsible? Yah! For instance, for some older men the shebeens can even provide such things as t-h-e-s-e,' pausing for me to look, then cupping his hands where 'bosoms' would be.

The husbands burst into guffaws. I was puzzled. Suddenly one shy wife piped up hotly: 'It's just another way to degrade us black people, Auntie, this legalisation!'

One husband collected himself and sighed, growling: 'Yes, Auntie, the Government knows what it's doing. Always exploits our weaknesses. Their special branch are ever in those shebeens, mingling, listening, reporting.' The lively uninvited added: 'They even buy drinks for people.'

It had taken me moments to assimilate all this. When the penny finally dropped, what could I say? What would you yourself have found to say? I was dumbfounded.

Perhaps unlike me, you wouldn't, in silence, have reached for another sip of pink gin.

20

An unexpected encounter

୫ଚ

18 MAY 1977

The other week I took a step further in my pilgrimage down Southern Africa which, as GBS might have said, is 'a black girl in search of her father' the late DDT and mother Nolwandle Jabavu.

Crossing the river from my mother's country, the Republic of South Africa, is to breathe again the air of my own mother country, having been born on Fort Hare Native College campus in 1919.

Grahamstown is where I now am. Associate fellow of Rhodes University Institute for the study of English in Africa and guest of Rhodes University Institute of Social and Economic Research in my capacity as researcher of documents and material for my projected biography of my father.

But we shall slaughter that mouse another day, 'siyakuyihlinza lompuku ngenye imini'. I'm purposely postponing that 'confab' because Rhodes unwittingly tossed me into an unexpected resuscitation of a significant event in my love life and I'm impelled to unburden myself.

Just imagine, at this university, of all unlikely places, the image of one of my very first lovers of 40 years ago and 6 000 miles away awaited me in the entrance hall of the guest cottage I've been allotted for my three months' stay here.

However, don't we Xhosa say 'Unyawo alunampumlo'? Literally, 'the foot has no nose', but metaphorically combining the ideas 'it's a small world' and 'you never know where fate will lead you'. In

Xhosa it also suggests (slightly mixing metaphors) 'blind foot-steps unexpectedly retracing themselves' – a portent of situations best left to your imagination.

On entering my guest cottage and before unpacking my tooth-brush, wigs, manuscripts, I inspected the prints adorning the walls. Yes. Typically 'English' behaviour!

The colour prints I examined were reassuring, the usual ones familiar to everybody: Oliver Cromwell, Elizabeth Fry, Vermeer's charming 'The Music Lesson'; Henry VIII as a Young Man, a Holbein. Well and good, my Rhodes pad was home from home.

But moving on, I suddenly beheld black and white prints that were new to me and I stopped. A print next to a map of Albany was a row of 'eminent 1820 settlers'. The name of one leapt at me. 'Rev William Shaw, 1798-1872.' The sight of the strong, handsome face confronted me with my lover of 40 years ago, 6 000 miles away! How come?

At about seventeen years old I was invited to a house party in Scotland, part of the coming out celebrations of a school chum.

Among my friend's guests was a hefty man called Shaw, about eighteen years old, well over six feet in his socks, whose family owned a neighbouring grouse shoot. A strong personality, he was one of the few who had known while still running around the playing fields he'd recently left what his career was to be. He was, as he said affectedly, 'Going for a soldier' at Sandhurst. We noted his decisiveness with respect.

On hearing I was from Cape Province, South Africa, he threw out that an eighteenth-century collateral relation of his had 'upped and gone for a missionary in those parts. Who knows? Possibly civilised your own people, Noni.'

The print on my Wall of Rev Shaw sparked me off on rapid re-searches. These confirmed the story we had youthfully scoffed at.

Indeed, the achievements were such as any kinsman direct or collateral may be proud of. I airmailed the news to my friend, informing him that among other attributes 'Rev WS has been a believer in education for the natives as the way to decent human relations'.

Now to strain your credulity further about my transfer to Rhodes. Several times in past years I've transferred myself from wherever I was to London to work, and rented a pad at Artillery Mansions, Artillery Row, SW1. My address here? It's in Artillery Road, RU! Has one's foot 'really really, nyani nyani' got no nose?

21

What kind of spouse?

🫖

25 MAY 1977

I might have known I'd put my foot in it when, writing about my impressions of the beautiful pagan people of Transkei, I burst out: 'Oh, to belong to a beautiful, bossy, ochre man!' I goofed by not spelling out: 'Joke. Don't take that too seriously.'

I discovered my mistake a few weeks later at a social gathering of my fellow 'school' Xhosa, which one described as 'of the elite'. (We southern blacks have developed a pronounced class conscious- ness during my 44 years away; we exceed the British only in that when gathered together we don't understate our exalted level, we actually remind ourselves of it.)

During the greetings and pleasantries, I was greatly teased about that joke in typically 'Xhosarised' English language exclamations: 'So, Noni, not satisfied with scolding we age mates of yours about our educated but scraped, shaven skulls, or our book-reading lethargy, you now "threaten falling in love with" a red ochre man? "Kulungile ke. All right then," shaking playful finger at me. 'We'll find you one "to fall in love with" and be your "baas". This author- ity you say you need.'

Being well aware of the thrusts underlying the joking, I said: 'Splendid: I do indeed adore the love and authority of a male boss – provided he orders me to do what I plan to do anyhow.'

Underneath the mutual leg-pulling, however, my thoughts were meandering. I was inwardly recalling how one day, admiring a resplendently attired pagan couple trudging past my hotel balcony, I had watched the lady being beckoned by her handsome authoritarian man to catch up while he stood still for her to remove something in his eye; doubtless a piece of grit, Umtata being one of the grittiest towns I've ever known.

She dutifully probed in his eye until suddenly, clap, wham. He dealt her cheek a resounding five-fingered backhander, then glowered down at her as she genuflected, eyes meekly cast down beneath her magnificent turban. 'Pig,' flashed through my mind. 'Is it ever possible to have one's eye probed without having to endure a modicum of discomfort?' Handsome pagan is as handsome does, but that was the sort of male authority I can do without.

As the social verbalising increased in volume from forte to fortissimo, I was noting yet again how surprisingly often I hear our educated southern blacks use that English phrase – 'to fall in love'. Uses of the English language here can be arresting; many phrases pertaining to love suggest concepts of the emotion that mystify, not to say frighten, me. I've overheard exclamations such as these: 'Maan. What a beautiful girl over there. I want to fall in love with her.' Or: 'What? You're advising me to be in love with that African man? Yuh. Never. I intend being in love with a European. Or Indian. A man to respect me, treat me nice. Not to grab my earnings.'

I've wondered about the actual emotional attitudes implied by such matter-of-fact expressions, what texture relationships.

Ancillary to this, I'd noticed a word that comes naturally, almost automatically, to Xhosa language speakers with reference to marriage partners, that subtle word 'owakwakhe'.

In tongues other than those of our great family of Bantu languages, one speaks of a husband or wife. 'Owakwakhe' seems to mean 'spouse of the homestead'; and the colloquialism refers to the female spouse as 'the one of the home'. If you're a woman who hasn't been brought up in a culture which has mores similar to those implied, then watch it girl when the next southern gentleman's gaze rests on your beauty.

I'm not the only Xhosa who, on experiencing the person-to-person aspect of being 'the one of the home', got out like a scalded cat. Some women, and I'm one of them, are so brought up that 'falling in love' is an inadvertent occurrence, no prior plan or intent. Where has the heart-throbbing emotion gone?

Having lived for several years on end in different countries with varied 'multinational identities', I have beheld or personally experienced a considerable range. So on hearing a southern black gentleman's reaction when the spectacle of a very pretty girl quickened him to, as he exclaimed, 'want to fall in love', I wondered, bearing in mind the status of 'the one of the home', whether his thoughts were meandering something like this: 'Might I not be blessed with quiverful upon quiverful of beautiful children from one so attractive? Might I not acquire a good – and thrifty – cook? Might she by chance possess a private income? Or have a degree, therefore a profession? But above all, most important' – and here my speculations were brushed by the memory of the gentleman with the grit in his eye – 'would she be obedient, behave herself and do as I say, or need the backhander or swish of the sjambok that keeps some ladies in line?'

It takes time to find your way around the jungles of mating procedures. But by now I've learned how to respond when some handsome 'blameless Ethiope' whispers manly sweet nothings in my ear. On the principle that what's sauce for the gander is nowadays sauce for the goose, too, this is what to do: give him your undivided attention, keep quiet and, if the declaration of passion suddenly turns into a question, answer with a smile only. Meanwhile, prepare to administer not the resounding backhander on the chauvinist cheek – too primitive – but the ice-cold shapely shoulder.

JUNE

June presents us with five columns held together by a thread: music. This is one of Noni's passions as she reflects on the different ways in which music has influenced her life. In the first column, 'The sound of music', she reflects on the global influences of her musical experiences while travelling to a variety of countries such as Cuba, Venezuela and the USA. The following week she writes about the varieties of music found in South Africa, referring to them as a rainbow to highlight the diverse sounds. The political thread is overt in the two seemingly unrelated columns which diverge from the theme of music: 'Petty apartheid 1977' and 'Three languages rich'. These distinct topics highlight the range of Noni's interests and the extent of her observation of the idiosyncrasies she does not fully understand in the South Africa she is trying to appreciate, despite the backdrop of apartheid laws.

ATHAMBILE MASOLA

22

The sound of music

୬ଚ

1 JUNE 1977

Having left my home on the Fort Hare campus when young and under the musical influence of my father, a fine musician as everyone remembers, I never forgot how he would smilingly chide us young people when we'd tell him that at such and such a 'tswari' (Xhosa derivation of the French 'soirée') we'd swayed to Mbaqanga, S'ponono, tiekie-draai – exceedingly primitive African tunes comprising only two beats, two notes to the bar, repeated ad infinitum.

Returning now two generations later, I confess I surreptitiously 'sway' to the seductive sound of tiekie-draai on the Xhosa radio programmes. Its possibilities have indeed been developed by some of the abler current black bands during the years I've been away. To hear it twangs at my heart strings; it's hard to conquer one's atavistic emotions.

Whenever I've lived among blacks in other lands, I've inwardly declared 'Hayi suka! These blacks can't sing as we Xhosa do at home.' Which was of course only marginally true, indeed irrational.

Years ago, living in Uganda and Kenya, I was spellbound by the natives' drumming. The performers were dedicated musicians, as were the makers of the different types of drums who selected, seasoned, and shaped the suitable type of logs of wood (for, so to say, a bass drum, a baritone or tenor drum, and so on), as were the craftsmen who cured the – to me – smelly cow or goat skins until satisfied they were perfect. So too the experienced makers of wind instruments out of ox or goat horns into wind instruments which accent the percussion section.

When my ears got used to the precise functions of tympani versus wind sections of these to me 'primitive' native orchestras, and I began to notice how the performers signalled one another by bulging sideways eye glances or nods of heads, I realised that they were not only obeying strict contrapuntal rules but were also signalling one or other virtuoso that it was his turn to improvise his solo. I noticed that the percussionists (the drummers) used not sticks, as on kettledrums, but parts of their amazingly flexible fingers, the palms and edges of their hands for subtly varied and intricate effects.

Then I lived for years in the West Indies, exposed to 'Calypso' music, to me a new genre. After my West Indian years, then the USA, there exposed to the blues.

On a brief visit to Cuba and Venezuela, I was exposed to the rhumba, samba and beguine, based on black 'primitive' but heavily adulterated by different types of so-called advanced civilised white music.

By the end of my years among Western hemisphere blacks, my irrational Xhosa musical chauvinism had mercifully gone 'out the window'. I became hooked on what would here in South Africa be called 'miscegenated' music.

At first a stranger among these West Indian and Afro-American blacks, only their joyful rhythms hit me. I 'swayed', danced, mindlessly happy. Later, beginning to distinguish between the dialects and idioms of their mother languages English or Spanish, I began to understand that the dialects varied not only from island to island but within districts of each island. To me this was an example of historical African 'tribalism'.

I became further spellbound, this time by the Calypso, that form of spontaneous music that the lyrics of which lampoon current political, national, sociological, historical events.

Life's experience for the West Indian black has been hard for centuries – slavery and all that. Therefore, understandably, their artistic emotions dwell on what philosophers call 'The Human Condition'.

Nations throw up an artistic giant now and again. Hence such great Calypsonians as 'The Mighty Sparrow', or 'Lord Kitchener', or 'The Roaring Lion'. Believe me or not, I was astonished on arriving in RSA last year to hear them being played on the Afrikaans programme. How could this be allowed? But no mention is made of the colour of foreign black musicians, so perhaps the Nats don't know how their identity is being polluted.

During my life among Western hemisphere blacks, I used to join the crowds who went to hear Sparrow, or Kitchener, or Lion. Even hurricanes didn't deter us. I was among those who participated, come heaven or hell weather (in Xhosa ndingafun' ukuphoswa, not wanting to miss anything) because did such occasions not constitute a sociological, historical, cathartic experience, a phenomenon peculiar to Western hemisphere blacks from which they gain refreshment, strength, courage, thus allowing their atavistic heart strings to be stirred.

A West Indian politician, black, Chinese, Indian or white, would feel his campaign diminished were his electioneering not lampooned by Calypsonians who sing about what they call 'These lying promises to raise de people (sic) standard of living while he self (sic) livin' on de fat o' de land, boy!'

I was reminded of this last year on arriving in South Africa in the wake of Soweto and being here during the subsequent unrest and crises up and down the land.

I have never seen pictures of Prime Minister Vorster or white politicians in power or opposition smiling as black politicians smile, whether meaning it or not during ceremonial or political election-eering. And in my naiveté as a daughter of Africa, I thought what splendid Calypsos Mighty Sparrow or Lord Kitchener would compose of such pronouncements as 'There's no crisis', or 'Squatters' shacks are not bulldozed, only humanely dismantled by hand'.

23

Republic's rainbow of music

ॐ

8 JUNE 1977

It would have made a cat laugh to see me trying to find my way around my radio when I arrived in South Africa.

One of the disadvantages of travelling alone in foreign countries if you don't understand about wavelengths and megahertzes and so on is having to twiddle and fiddle with the knobs looking for music.

My RSA radio listening began in Natal, where I spent several weeks and acquired a portable South African radio set labelled FM and SW. I'd no idea what FM meant, never having seen one before. So, fiddling and twiddling its knobs, I found some gorgeous classical music, a veritable feast. The explanatory announcements were in a language that sounded foreign to my ears and which was spoken in soft, cultured tones.

Later, I asked my hosts about these programmes: were they from a French-speaking country such as Madagascar or the Seychelles, or Mozambique? (Even if you are a French speaker as I am, you are not necessarily conversant or fluent in its colonial dialects.)

When my Natal hosts told me that the programme I had found and enjoyed was the Afrikaans programme, I nearly fell off my chair.

Recovering, I asked: 'Do you mean the Boers are cultured people nowadays?' My hosts smiled at me in a mixture of pity, affection and amusement, saying: 'Sis' Noni, you are due for many surprises in this South Africa of yours after so long away. One such surprise is that nowadays a very big section of amaBhunu (my hosts were Zulu speakers) are civilised now.' Yet their teenage son, the age of one of my grandsons, was at that moment imprisoned somewhere by the Boers in power, under Section 6. Detained. No explanation given, no visits allowed.

On coming further south, twiddling away at my radio bedmate, I wondered why I didn't hear any Afrikaans choir singing? For on the English and Xhosa programmes I heard lots of breathtaking choir singing, the music being from both cultures, Xhosa or European (Bach, Beethoven, etc).

An odd thing about some languages is that you may not enjoy hearing them spoken, but hearing them sung will take you to heaven's gates. I, for instance, don't much like to hear German spoken but to hear it sung, its beauty makes me nearly faint. I don't much like to hear Afrikaans spoken, but I guess I might feel elevated if I heard it sung. Classical Afrikaans music, I mean.

On the English programme, I've been overjoyed by the music provided by Dolores Mather-Pike. Her name took me back to my short time at the Royal Academy of Music in London, where my contemporaries and friends had similarly lovely names: two violinists Hermione Spencer-Killick and Anne Tierny, who played duets; Olive Zorian, Joy Hall, Dennis Brain, the Catterall brothers, Alexander Timberlake and many others.

I was lucky enough to have a small grand piano in my flat near the Academy, so they used to come for tea and to make music. My great friend was a Pretorian, Margery Choles. She introduced me to Bach's 'Art of Fugue'. She talked about a South African composer called Arnold van Wyk. One day as I twiddled my set, I caught something by this Arnold van Wyk and thus remembered my South African white friend, Margery Choles. How I'd love to meet her again, if only whites and blacks were not discouraged in their friendships.

As a schoolgirl in York, England, among the instrumentalists who performed for us were the cellist Carl Fuchs and the violinists Adela Fachiri and her sister, Jelly d'Aranyi. I've since heard them on the Afrikaans programme. Truly, wonders never cease.

Of course, in South Africa even music is supposed to be white, black, Indian or coloured. Isn't it amazing music? Rainbow.

24
Petty apartheid 1977

࿐

The new, to me, phrases that embellish the speeches of my mother country's official representatives nowadays have been much on my mind. 'Multi-national', 'plural societies', 'multiple democracies', 'homelands', 'separate but equal'; eye-opening pronouncements about how nobody in our country need any longer quarrel about entrances, lifts, loos, labelled in colours of ethnicities. Why? Because communists and Cubans are staring us in the face. Fate worse than death, worse than apartheid.

'Petty apartheid no longer exists.' If, like me, you are black and have been away for generations, such phrases confound and confuse you, particularly if you are considerably older than Pik – I mean Mr RF you-know-who, as he now prefers to be called.

On the radio I've listened to Mr Pik Botha expressing his views on petty apartheid and on Mr Andrew Young and my grey wig involuntarily shook from side to side because he shouts, positively rants. Incidentally, I've met both Pik and Andy at Washington DC receptions and they seemed quite chummy together then.

But elderly ladies digress, don't they?

To recall petty apartheid in South Africa as it was 20-odd years ago, I quote a passage from my book, *The Ochre People*: '"Sorry I am late, grandmother," the young girl said to my aunt on arriving out of breath at my old aunt's Pimville Location house. "It was the railway clerk who has delayed me for your errands. That Boer ticket

117

seller was in one of those funny moods of his, when he decides to read his newspaper from cover to cover, slowly, occasionally looking up scornfully at our queue of black people anxious to buy-ticket, catch-train to work. He reads oh so slowly. We wait and wait. At last some can't continue waiting on his pleasure and we go. So, I too, today have walked the six miles to help you out, rather than wait until that Boer felt like doing his job of selling tickets to us black people. Sorry, Grandmother."'

'Grandmother listened quietly. She in her late seventies was restraint personified. I felt like exploding; but her presence commanded my restraint too. My generation were brought up to control our indignation, our rebelliousness. Were we perhaps too properly brought up?'

That was from the 1950s. Now I tell petty apartheid like it is in 1977, from a passage in the book I'm writing about my return to South Africa 20 years later:

'I wished to travel in 1976 from a country station in Natal by SAR [South African Railways], first class, to Cape Town. At the Nie-Blankes ticket hatch, the young Afrikaner ticket seller wrote out my ticket. There was plate-glass window between us, naturally. So, while I wrote, I read a brass metal plaque on my side of the window which enjoined passengers to examine their ticket before passing their fare through the hatch because mistakes would not later be rectified. I then looked around, observing detail as one does, while he wrote. He finished then looked up at me with scowling face, demanded the fare, which was scores of rands, of course. I held in my hand for him to see, a wad of several hundreds of rands. As he stared at it, I said in my middle-aged, gentle tones: "Would you please turn what you've written around for me to examine it? I'm not good at reading things upside down." He glared at me. I repeated and added: "Your writing is facing you, isn't it? For me it's upside down. I'd like to read and examine, that's all."

'The young man stood motionless, if not to say riveted, focusing eyes on me which were in expression, the epitome of: "If looks could kill." I became irritated and returned his black look with my own blazing eyes. Upon which he turned his back on me, leaned on a chair, crossed his well-shaped long legs, fumbled in his pocket for cigarette and lighter, and gazed out at the view. Silence. Talk about a deathly hush all over the world. I looked round at the fellow blacks queuing behind me who watched the scene. They were an audience electrified with anxiety. So, I smiled to put them at ease, then turned again to the spectacle of the well-built, broad-shouldered young Afrikaner clerk's shoulders. He was taking deep breaths on his cigarette. So, I said quietly, exercising my privilege of age: "Listen to me, young fellow, I doubt if your parents would like to see how you're behaving just now. On duty but paying no attention to your duty. You're paid to work. You're not doing your work. You see that I do indeed have the money to pay for this huge fare. Why are you behaving like this? Do you think I have more money than a native is supposed to possess? Jealous, is that it? You may be mistaken. Appearances are not always what they seem. Probably you have more money than me, my dear. I'll light up my own fag now, while you smoke yours, until you are prepared to do your work."

'Talk about scathing, biting, reddened claws, adrenalin pumping. The more quietly you do these horrible things, the more effective. I saw the backs of the young Afrikaner clerk's ears turn scarlet, almost mauve, purple. My own face was red hot, my fingers trembling. I was afraid I might collapse in a faint. I tightened myself . . .

'After a wait of nearly an hour, he and I completed our job in the spirit of separate but equal, of apartheid, of hate, loathing.

Meanwhile, I chiding myself inwardly: "Why get cross with a youngster of this type? Maybe he's the product of a broken Afrikaner home, poor child, and his behaviour could be a psychological cry for help in the world of confusion in which he finds himself. Lucky me, my grandchildren overseas who are the same age and all of them, 'multicoloured, multinational, plural genetic and ethnics' are not sorry spectacles like this young boy."

'What went through my mind as I walked away from the Nie-Blankes SAR ticket hatch were thoughts like these: Discrimination, petty apartheid, 1955, 1977, Pik Botha? Plus ça change, plus c'est la même chose . . ." Something like that.

'Except that our lovely subcontinent of Southern Africa is now surrounded by communists, ruthless coloureds from the island of Cuba.'

Here I end my quote from my forthcoming book. One of these Wednesdays, I hope to talk about other things and perhaps cheer us both up.

25

Music to learn by

22 JUNE 1977

Doh Ray Mee. Tonic sol-fa. The fist for Doh, the first finger pointed upright for Ray, the hand levelled for Mee.

Isn't that the way we were taught to sing at school? For example, when I was a day scholar at Lovedale? Some of my former teachers whom I met when I was in Umtata gathering material for my father's biography said to me: 'Nontando, in your book about Jili (my father's clan name), don't leave out his music-making, his choir mastership.'

Well, at home, more than 40 years ago in my parents' house at Fort Hare, we had our piano, a wedding present to my parents from friends in England. So, I learned staff notation, but at school I also learned tonic sol-fa.

It was only recently that I learned the origin of the tonic sol-fa system, and I'd like to share it with you. It was invented by an Italian born in the year 995 AD, called Guido d'Arezzo – or if you Latinists prefer his Latin surname, 'Aretinus'. He was born in Paris and became a monk of great learning. He introduced the hexachord system, which is a group of six notes suitable for singing at sight. And this form of sight-reading embodied the main principle of the tonic sol-fa as we now know it.

Before that, people had to learn music by heart. The system was perfected in the 19th century by a minister of the Congregational Church, John Curwen, who founded a music publishing firm which is still going and which bears his name.

The system spread rapidly all over the world, especially in countries where pianos were not available and choirs needed to learn a new song rapidly. Tonic sol-fa was the answer to their difficulty. God's gift.

Now, my father was a splendid choirmaster. This is not filial loyalty or filial pride. (I've discovered that he was a naughty man, too, like me. But my discoveries of skeletons in family cupboards are material for my book, not for weekly columns.)

When King George VI and his family came to South Africa in 1947, my father was asked by the Ciskei black and white people to conduct choirs to sing for the King and Queen and the young princesses. There was a lovely picture in a newspaper of my father and King George – my father holding one arm up high and the King, in profile, laughing his head off, so much so that you could see his back teeth – and King George VI was a shy man as everyone knows. But my father was a Sidney Smith type, the 18th-century gentleman who could make everybody laugh and be happy.

(And may I digress from music to ask if any 60-year-old age mate of mine has that newspaper picture? And if so, would he or she lend it to me to be reproduced? I promise to return it.)

When I was about sixteen or seventeen, there was to be a concert at the location Ntselamanzi, in the hall which my parents' friend, the Hon Alexandra Peckover of Cambridge, had donated all of the money for.

I and a schoolgirl friend practised some songs at my home as our contribution to the concert. An untrained singer, she was possessor of one of the most beautiful, liquid soprano voices anyone can ever hope to hear. My classmate in Std V, Rosalie Gqomfa was her name. I was her accompanist on the piano, and we perfected everything on my parents' Broadwood upright piano at our home at Fort Hare College, as it then was.

Came the night of the concert at Ntselamanzi. Rosalie stood up to sing. I sat at the Ntselamanzi Hall piano to accompany her. But, oh gosh, the piano had not been tuned, serviced, by the tuner who had promised the month before to do the job.

So, Rosalie and I were stranded until my father, DDTJ, came to the rescue. He said to us in his fatherly voice: 'My dear children, Rosalie and Nontando, don't worry yourselves. Something is not quite right with this piano. Let me help.' By that, this beautiful father of mine meant that he would accompany Rosalie, sight reading (in very bad light, only a candle) and transposing from different keys!

What wonderful people I am descended from. Forgive me, but I must pay homage to them.

26
Three languages rich

🕊

29 JUNE 1977

Languages. Aren't they interesting to use? I possess a working knowledge of several. By 'working' I mean not necessarily grammatical, only to understand and be understood.

Here in South Africa I use three languages, English, Xhosa and Afrikaans. All are important, so much so that one has to talk about them in their alphabetical order.

Have you Afrikaans speakers noticed how your language has developed and grown in scope? And been influenced by your environment as Africans in Africa? It's a most expressive tribal language. Let me whisper something to you which I hope will make you laugh about Afrikaans:

During my travels up and down this lovely country of ours, at railway stations and so on I've had to stare at these apartheid signs to try and avoid making mistakes. So, I keep seeing the sign 'Nie-Blankes' and I did get the message. But in my English way, I pronounced it 'Nyer-Blanks'.

My Boer friends nearly died laughing and explained to me that in Afrikaans there's a big difference in the meaning of 'nyer' and 'nie'. I should pronounce it 'knee' as in Negro, knee-grow.

It was my own turn to fall down in amazement. Why? Because my children and grandchildren (my American ones) absolutely loathe, hate, being called 'knee-grows'. When I'm visiting them, I have to refer to 'Nie-Blankes' as 'Afro-Americans'.

May I refer to you, my Afrikaans-speaking friends, as 'Nie-Swartes?'

Now then, English language speakers. My goodness, what a variety of accents we use, not only in South Africa, but all over the world. For this is a world language, not a tribal language, and therefore arouses different and very exciting interests and emotions.

Have you noticed how class-biased in language we are? When I listen to, say, Eastern Cape Settler English speakers, I have to force myself to remember that they aren't at all 'low class' despite ridiculous words like 'goodies'. Their speech has been influenced by Afrikaans and Xhosa. It's my grandchildren who would ridicule them, not me. I'm a linguist by birth, not by training. (I don't possess a degree in English, I only speak it.)

My Afro-American grandchildren and my English grandchildren in England whose playmates are young dukes and twelfth earls and honourables – let alone young marquesses and lords – their accents or tones fascinate my ears. And I notice how ruthless these young ones are towards one another's accents.

But I keep quiet while listening to them. My friend Robert Graves gave me that piece of advice: 'Use your ears, Noni. Don't talk. Reflect later in tranquillity, the messages your ears received . . .'

Now let's talk about Xhosa, one of the strongest of the great family of Bantu languages.

I've said that one of the things that struck me most on my return to South Africa is the unexampled vigour with which southern blacks do what they enjoy doing. (We can be jolly lazy when it comes to doing something we don't enjoy doing.) Using our Xhosa language and adapting it to our changing world is something we do with all our strength, and how amusingly we do it.

Listen: many of us nowadays suffer from high blood pressure because we so love to eat. We now have a word for this complaint.

We say: I have got this 'high high', and we fall about laughing as we make the announcement.

It is almost an affectionate term, isn't it? Yes, for it's easier to cope affectionately with an enemy.

The young ones are fond of partaking in brain quizzes and they call them 'peel grey matter', 'cubha ubuchopho'.

Deodorants are much in use among us nowadays. Guess what we call them? 'izibulala-vumba': 'smell killers'.

And because we eat with unexampled vigour, we are prone to indigestion. So, we hand the sufferer one or other of numerous salts which are alleged to cure the condition. And because we are not a shy, embarrassed type of linguist, guess what we say in Xhosarised English? We say: 'Drink it, it will relieve you, make you burp. Like this,' and you burp loudly, with vigour, to show how you will obtain relief.

Is this not a strong, growing language indeed? I had believed, as a Kiswahili speaker, that Swahili is the seventh greatest language of the world. But I have demoted it now for I've found that Xhosa is greater in the sense of stronger, more adaptable.

South Africa is fortunate and unique in possessing Afrikaans for it's a splendid tribal language, and English which is a splendid commercial language, and Xhosa, the strongest of the 400 or more Bantu languages on our continent.

We South Africans have much to be proud of in possessing our unique languages, neh? Not so? Akunjalo?

JULY

❧

'Xhosa language possesses great power of prose, prosaic expression of imagery, of emotional feelings.' In her typical storytelling style, Noni's first column in July focuses on the uses of words, on how social contexts, including whether the language is the speaker's mother tongue or not, prescribe which words are used and how. Noni also compares isiXhosa to English and notes how English '. . . is an exceedingly imprecise, adaptable language . . .'

'Let me talk about my friend Nat King Cole. The blackest of black men, the most courteous and kind and handsome that you could ever meet. Milk-white teeth when he smiles.' In the column 'Blues tell the story', Noni writes about her connection to and love for music, the various genres observed, the people as the makers of the music, particularly Black people of the world that she had travelled, and their connections to their roots. Noni's knowledge and passion for music pulsates palpably throughout this second column, which ends in the following way: 'By miscegenating, we develop. We grow. Our music-making develops, grows. What more can I say?'

'. . . I am a Black European, not a South African European.' Noni often had to explain herself when she returned to South Africa. She wrote about how on many occasions, she was misunderstood. This is one of the devastating impacts of institutionalised apartheid on the social lives of Black people. The debilitating 'tribalisation' through laws and insistence on Black people occupying their own 'homelands' was a deliberate attempt at policing and controlling

Black people, and thus it limited their perspectives. Noni's third and last columns in July, 'Love, law and languages' and 'Enter the ENT specialist...', are both critiques of apartheid and assertions of her own identity.

Communication and/or engagement thus summarise the theme of her columns in July: human interactions through languages, music and love and how these unfold. The same themes, she suggests, contribute to one's perception of one's own identity.

MAKHOSAZANA XABA

27
Different languages to fit the occasion

಩

6 JULY 1977

Although I said recently that we South Africans may pride ourselves on our possession of the languages Afrikaans, English and Xhosa, I have to say something different today.

Those of us who speak all three – or more, for instance, Sotho speakers and speakers of the different dialects of Afrikaans, English, Zulu – have problems.

Some of these difficulties are based on social class differences. For example, when I had to spend some months in Natal the year before last, a conversation in the house came round to the subject of hijacked airplanes. This was in the wake of the Israeli rescue of the hijacked plane at Entebbe.

Everyone present exclaimed. Everyone was a Zulu and English-language speaker except me. I could only communicate with them in English about my own experience of having been in an airplane that had been hijacked. Those present were aghast and asked: 'What was it like, Noni?'

I replied truthfully: 'It was fascinating.' Everyone gaped and gasped. It was the word 'fascinating' which fascinated the company.

I only realised their reaction because they kept quoting it back to me and to one another. Clearly it was an amazing word to use in that context, in that company.

Yet it's a very ordinary use of it in certain social classes in England: the so-called upper classes and upper middle classes.

What I found puzzling me as I listened to these Bantu language speakers was their constant confusion of the words 'he' and 'she'. The imprecision was, for me, nerve-wracking to the ears. My own use of certain English words, combined with what they called my 'tone', was puzzling to them.

Why did their own use of the English language puzzle and annoy my nerves and ears?

Illogically, because English is an exceedingly imprecise, adaptable language; therefore, also the most capable of poetic expression.

The Xhosa language possesses great power of prose, prosaic expression of imagery, of emotional feelings.

I don't know yet what is the great gift of the Afrikaans language. I'll have to hear it sung. Classical Afrikaans religious choir music, if any exists.

To me, the German language when spoken is not very pleasing. But when sung by a Bach choir it is pure heaven.

Is there an Afrikaans equivalent of JS Bach? If so, may I meet him? To talk about the problems of librettos, how to overcome them?

For language, the use of, is a great thing.

28

Blues tell the story

๛

More than once you've read that one of the things I've missed about my mother country during my Rip Van Winkle absence is the vigour with which my black people do anything they truly enjoy doing.

Making music is one of their supreme things. Yuh, engomeni abantu abamnyama? In song, music? The people truly abandon themselves, bayazinikela.

Blacks all over the world. I've spoken of my years among our blacks of the Western hemisphere, West Indians, Afro-Americans. Of how the music they make is vigorous beyond compare and has, as everyone knows, influenced the music of the globe with the blues, or the 'bloos', as they pronounce it.

You know the structure of a blues, the twelve-bar blues, the eight-bar blues. I've been amazed to hear the blues played even in South Africa and the Soviet Union; in countries whose powerful rulers do all they can to prevent what they call 'the cultural pollution of their white ethnic identities'.

Go to an Afro-American church or a South African black church, a Rhodesian black church and the music the worshippers make knocks you out. You'll hear Aretha Franklins, Mahalia Jacksons, Ray Charleses, BB Kings, Lena Hornes, Louis Armstrongs – right here in South Africa if you can obtain a permit to visit a black location. But you will be lucky to get one. If you succeed, you'll see for yourself how black music is absolutely rooted in their religion and their religious music.

They live it daily. Their music speaks of joy, happiness, pain, love, hate, disillusion, the ancestors. To say nothing of black jazz composers. What Afrikaner hasn't heard of Duke Ellington or of Nat King Cole?

Let me talk about my friend Nat Cole. The blackest of black men, the most courteous and kind and handsome that you could ever meet. Milk-white teeth when he smiled.

Nat and his two other artistes (they were a trio as you will remember) came to my house near Buckingham Palace, Victoria Station, after giving their concert at a hall nearby. I cooked. We ate. Then Nat walked over to my piano, made a few notes testing, then turned round, smiling, and signalled the other two saying 'Straighten Up and Fly Right'.

They moved I tell you, bashukuma mfondini.

When they finished, Nat told me the history of the blues they had just played, explaining it was an ancestral folk tale from slave days.

'A tiny mouse was swooped upon by an eagle. Eagle powerful, mouse weak and helpless.

'But eagle he not too bright. Mouse, he got brains so he say to he-self: "Ah doan wanna die just yet. I must use my wits." So, mouse he squeak and say: "Eagle, straighten your claws boy and fly right on to get home quicker, eh?"

'Eagle he plenty hungry by now, so to get home quick and eat the mouse was like a good idea. So, he opened his claws.

'Mr Mouse, he drop and scuttle off. Mr Eagle, he fly straight on and that was that.'

There was a pause, so I jumped up saying: 'Nat, please excuse me. My little boy. Don't you hear him crying? He wants to be with us.'

Nat said: 'OK. Bring him.'

When I returned, my grandson in my arms, crying no more, Nat was practising, making arpeggios on my baby grand.

When I entered, Nat turned round, stood up and strode across to help me. A tall man, over six feet in height, Nat held my grandson for a minute or two, then gave him back to me. He walked to the piano, signalled the other two. They raised their instruments and Nat a commanding forefinger. He growled in that lovely baritone voice he had: 'Route 66'.

They moved into the blues, twelve bar. Nat's impeccable use of piano dynamics captivated not only me but my new-born grandson who listened with utter concentration, rolling his beautiful, great brown 'coloured' eyes. It seemed as if the little fellow understood what Nat was singing about.

Route 66 is one of the US national roads, 2 000 miles from east to west, criss-crossing the great and lovely country, mountains, plains, deserts . . .

Nat mentions the topography, the towns, the cities you pass as you drive on Route 66. Expressing all the emotions of the heart that a native-born feels for his country.

What Nat Cole sang about was the inheritance, ancestral roots. Are you an anthropologist, sociologist, psychiatrist? If so, you know what these things mean. Blacks have the inherited ability to express these emotions in their music-making. The so-called whites have been influenced by our music-making, so have the Japanese, Russians, Afrikaners.

We all interact on one another. We do miscegenate culturally. What's wrong with that?

By miscegenating, we develop. We grow. Our music-making develops, grows. What more can I say?

29
Love, law and languages

๛

20 JULY 1977

Last night in bed, I was planning to chat about regional accents in the many languages we are so fortunate to possess in this lovely country of ours ...

But I am somewhat confused. Why? My frank answer is: I've fallen in love. Isn't this love a difficult business? One has to force oneself not to think about it; to put it on the shelf, to feel free to chat with friends like yourselves who don't necessarily love me, for you have your own loves – neh, akunjalo, not so? ...

So, forget about my personal affection, my lover. (Yes, he loves me too, this South African! We haven't slept together. We can't. We are not allowed, not unless and until Mr Vorster makes some kind of a change in the law of the land. I wonder if he has listened to the advice from Mr RF Botha and Mr Hendrik Schoeman?) ...

So, we should chat about regional accents instead of our love lives ... love we can talk about another Wednesday.

In South Africa, languages are so many, so plentiful. Each of us has to use at least three, or even four of them.

Let's take them in alphabetical order. Afrikaans comes first, then English, then Sesuthu, Xhosa, Zulu.

Alas, my Afrikaans is somewhat primitive! So, let's leave it out. Sesuthu and Zulu I have none; I am a Fingo speaker of the Xhosa language. Proper Xhosa people don't like my Fingo accent. Ask the prince, duke, paramount chiefs of Transkei. They'll confirm that they don't like to hear an accent such as mine.

So, let's talk about English-language regional accents as used or inherited by white South Africans. I met white South Africans in great numbers only in 1975 and 1976. Before that, I'd had the opportunity to meet them only abroad – overseas; in Italy, Egypt, the United States, Central America, the West Indies. In those countries, they were able to visit me in my house. There are no laws against multiracial friendships in those countries.

Indeed, no other country in the world operates such beastly laws as the Immorality Act of South Africa, which aims at preventing God's children from befriending one another. It is splendid that Mr Botha and Mr Schoeman have made public suggestion that the Republic should drop this inhuman law and thus get into line with Western democracies.

I sincerely hope that Mr Botha and Mr Schoeman will succeed in persuading their fellow Nationalists to adopt this civilised outlook. Why? Because none of us will lose our identities by being free to meet one another.

Indeed, South Africa is one of the unique countries in the world for possessing so many interesting cultures, languages and accents, which all of us use or have inherited in speaking these languages in the far-flung regions of our lovely mother country.

It's only recently that I've had the chance to listen to and analyse them, because I've been away for something like two generations.

In 1975 I came back home to South Africa to visit my parents' and brother's and sister's graves. I was followed by members of the Special Branch right into my late father's house at Middledrift. The two gentlemen pretended they were not Special Branch. I kept quiet to listen to their accents.

How interesting these proved to be! The word 'still' came out of their moustached lips as 'st'l'; the word 'yes' came out as 'yiss'; 'light'; came out as 'laht'; 'car park' as 'caw pawk'.

'Which political pawty do you favour, Miss Jabavu?'

I stared, because I didn't understand what he meant by 'pawty'. As for 'politics' that's never been my scene. My friends who went into politics, such as Gen. Smuts, Mrs Indira Ghandi, Mohan Kumaramangalam, Winston Churchill (the grandson), all were braver than I.

For I am concerned only with, and write books only about, human affection, love, jealousies, reconciliations. I said as much. But the Special Branch gents were puzzled by my accent, my 'tone'; they stared back at me!

So, I rose and ushered them out on to the verandah, to gaze at the view of the Amatola mountain range. (This was my English manner of asking them to leave me.) But as they were Afrikaners, they could hardly understand what I meant because their accent puzzled me! Why did it prove puzzling to me? Because the Government has prevented South Africans from visiting one another ever since 1948.

30

Enter the ENT specialist . . .

ಅೞ

27 JULY 1977

'Depend upon it, Sir, when a man knows he is to be hanged in a fortnight, it concentrates his mind wonderfully.'

So said Dr Johnson, but exercising our Xhosa manners, we natives would courteously refer to him as Father Doctor – uTata Gqirha Johnson.

Today I'm saying something like this: 'Depend upon it, Sir, when a black girl returns to her mother country the Republic of South Africa after an absence of a couple of generations, even when not about to be hanged, the experience concentrates her mind wonder-fully in very many directions.'

It has made me wish that I were, among other things, an Ear, Nose and Throat specialist.

Why? Let's take the ear first. I mean the ethnic ear of white South Africans. What an admirable physiological instrument it has turned out to be in its adaptation to the enormous noise that native South Africans make when merely conversing with each other! The white South African organ of hearing has truly adapted to accommodate itself to its environment.

I say this because during my long visit, a motion was discussed in the white House of Assembly about providing places of wor-ship on a Sunday for natives who work for whites in towns and cities. The motion created an uproar within the ruling ethnic class. The Deputy Minister of Bantu Administration and Education,

Dr Treurnicht, opposed it, saying in effect that black ethnics have their own churches in their locations, and implied that the Government's view was that natives may not pray to our God in a Group Area which is not their own ethnic Group Area. (Doesn't this word ethnic begin to sound peculiar, almost like a four-letter word? But brother, you have to get used to it in South Africa!)

In the rash of correspondence that broke out in newspapers up and down the land was one letter which touchingly summed up the feelings of some Christian white South Africans. The writer pleaded: 'Blacks are not forbidden from making as much noise as they like talking to each other as they work in our areas during the week. So why may they not kneel and be quiet for an hour of worship on a Sunday?'

I was astonished to realise that white South Africans are accustomed to and accept the dreadful noise that we natives make in conversation. My own black ear, being more 'European' than that of white South Africans, absolutely cannot abide the noise my people make. I was brought up in England, where I lived for over 40 years. My white British ethnic servants knew better than to talk above a whisper while working for me. And in Kenya where I've lived for over eleven years and in the West Indies where I lived for something like six years, my servants – ethnically blacks and browns – were jolly well trained by us British expatriates to be as quiet as mice. Were I to settle in this lovely South Africa, I would jolly well do my own housework, cooking, gardening, everything.

You ask why. I answer: 'Because my fellow natives are too dashed noisy!' You riposte: 'But rich people like you Europeans, Noni, it's your duty to employ us poor people.'

I'm not inventing these dialogues. They took place very often between me and South Africans. I reply: 'Much as I'd like to give jobs, I wouldn't do it. My ear cannot adapt itself, for I am a black European, not a South African European.'

Jaws drop, eyes open, loud laughter breaks out. I purse my lips. 'European' style. Then while everyone is gigitheka-ing (lovely Xhosa word meaning killing themselves with laughter), I continue: 'Not only noisy. We ethnic people are so nosey, so curious, inquisitive! And white South Africans too.'

Now here's where my specialisation on the nose comes in.

In every location, Bantustan, town, city I lived in during my year in South Africa, I found members of all ethnic groups incredibly nosey. I've been chased up streets by blacks shouting to me to stop. I stopped thinking it must be something urgent – maybe I'd let fall a R10 note . . .

Gasping for breath, the shouter would shake my hand and end up saying: 'I've been seeing you around so often – who are you, where do you come from?' My turn to gasp, surprised, somewhat offended. 'Is it your business?' 'Well, no, heh heh! But I want to know for I seldom see so pretty a girl as you!'

Well, I softened momentarily. One doesn't often receive such compliments. So, I smiled – wouldn't you? But the European part of me doesn't submit to nosiness easily. I said: 'Thank you, mama. I'm afraid I can't stop and talk. I'm en route to the bank. It's about to close right now.' I thus shake off this particular black nosey nose.

Into the bank to collect my draft from London. The manager, a white South African meeting me for the first time, necessarily examines my identification documents. My passport says: 'Place of birth, Fort Hare, CP, South Africa. Date 20 August 1919.'

His eyes open: his well-shaped, high-bridged nose quivers with interest and noses away at its job. The ears flap, astounded by my English accent which of course I can't help. We take something like a whole hour in friendly civilised chat – like a typical South

African he, too, wants to know all about me. But he can use subtler tactics.

My South African white bank managers up and down the land knew better than to chase me up streets, for they knew about the Immorality Act. But behind closed doors interviewing me over several pots of tea, explaining about exchange rates due to devaluation, all of which I don't understand and therefore could merely smile at, these courteous gentlemen could indulge their curiosity to their hearts' content – bless them all.

It occurred to me as I watched that they were members of a typical African tribe. An industrialised, commercial one of course. They too, have adapted to the environment, but don't need to open their throats and shout while working or in conversation . . .

Which brings me to the throat part of my concentrated specialisation.

Have you noticed how birds as nestlings use their throat? So wide open, you wonder they don't tear the corners of their beaks. Wide, wider, widest, so that food may be stuffed down. The instant it's swallowed, wide open again singing for more!

Ethnic blacks are, as we all know, tremendous openers of throats. But this must be an environmental characteristic, not an inherited one. For I, black as I am, was forced to actually learn the art of opening my throat and using my neck and jaw muscles. By whom? By my Professor of Singing at the Royal Academy of Music in London, just before World War II broke out.

The British ethnic environment I was reared in militated against opening one's throat – let alone one's teeth – or shouting when talking. So, my friends and I were sent to expensive academies to be taught how to produce and project our God-given voices, just as many babies have to be taught how to suck their mothers' nipples.

140

I was greatly surprised when one of my own babes had to be so taught. Indeed, I became furious with the white doctor, matron and midwives of the nursing home at which I gave birth for I mistakenly thought they were mistreating the little creature as they manipulated the tiny neck muscles!

But in South Africa I noticed that each and every ethnic group has adapted itself to the environment, to one another. Their ears, noses and throats have got it to a 't'.

AUGUST

Like March, June and November, August presents us with five columns. 'Law I hate, books I like' is a two-part column as Noni writes about two seemingly unrelated issues: apartheid laws and her love for books. Noni uses her personal experience with South Africa's apartheid laws and the consequences it had on her relationships and travels. While she writes about her jarring experiences of being home in a country she cannot fully recognise, she intersperses her commentary with her experience of living in Kenya and the liberties she enjoyed in the country of her choice.

'When the sky didn't fall' shows that Noni is in conversation with her readers who constantly write letters in response to her columns. She engages their ideas and challenges them by pointing out the ways in which people have accepted apartheid laws as a norm that should not be challenged, showing them the ways in which it is possible to challenge segregation because the sky won't fall if they do. Noni is aware that her privilege to travel and see and experience places such as France and Switzerland allows her the ability to see South Africa from a different perspective. The thread in this month's columns isn't immediately obvious when looking at the titles; however, Noni continues to demonstrate that the personal is political.

ATHAMBILE MASOLA

31

Law I hate, books I like

ﻌﻌ

3 AUGUST 1977

If you had been away from your mother country for longer than a lifetime, two lifetimes, as I myself have been, there are some things that would surprise or hurt you deeply.

The Group Areas Act . . . When I arrived back in 1975 and again in 1976, I coincided with the arrivals from England of three of my closest friends. Such close people to me you could call them – as I call them in Xhosa, abantu bam, my people – for they are my white mother, her son and our friend who is an English actress.

None of us was aware of the Group Areas Act, let alone what it would mean to us as individuals. How we learned our lesson was like this, and deeply hurtful and humiliating:

My 'white' mother is Lady Norman, widow of Lord Montagu, the Chairman of the Bank of England during the 1930s. I am her 'black' daughter. Our connection was through the banking world. When I was a young child in England at that time, I was in that world, through no fault of my own!

Lady Norman, my mother who gave me permission to call her by her name Priscilla, and one of her sons, Peregrine Worsthorne (who is therefore my 'brother' Perry), and our friend Moyra Fraser whose husband was my close friend a lifetime ago before she married him, were unable to meet me when we coincidentally found ourselves in South Africa. Why?

Because in South Africa we are classified under one or other of the sections of the Group Areas Act as 'black' or 'white'. We are different, ethnically, and therefore not allowed to sleep in the same house or eat together at the same table . . . let alone be seen through the window of some restaurant eating at the same table by a law enforcement officer.

The duty of a South African policeman is to see that Christians of different ethnic groups, colours, don't mix, don't do anything together. They must be apart at all times.

So, Priscilla Norman, her son Peregrine Worsthorne, Moyra Fraser and Noni Jabavu were unable to see each other in this Republic of South Africa which is Noni's mother country. We were not allowed, for it is against the National Party's law.

How about that! So, we had to wait until we were in a different Western Christian Democratic country, in which God rules a different law and allows His children to behave according to His rules. It is only in the Republic of South Africa that Priscilla, Moyra, Noni and Peregrine are not allowed to mix.

*

If you are a writer, as I am, you cannot understand how people who wish to write books, or say they could if they had the time, don't read books!

To read books is the life and drink of a writer who means business. Even if you don't publish a book for a long time, as I myself haven't, you must continue to read and read. You absolutely have to. You can't help yourself – otherwise you might as well stop breathing!

I usually read and reread two novels by Arnold Bennett, *The Old Wives' Tale* and *Clayhanger*. Magnificent books. So jolly, humorous and such wonderful observation of human behaviour.

The older you get, the more you learn from rereading them

every year. And I am jolly elderly now, nearer 60 than sixteen, so you can understand that I need and am getting sustenance from Arnold Bennett's novels.

Also, of course, I read my Concise English Dictionary, my Swahili Dictionary, my Xhosa Grammar books by my grandfather's friend McLaren.

Those are my staple diet. But what am I reading now, you ask? I'm devouring *The Frank Muir Book* which is subtitled: *An irreverent companion to social history.* Have you dipped into it? If not, why not? We South Africans should learn more than we know about our social circumstances. The only way we can do this is by reading such books as this.

And guess what else? My father's biography of his father: *The Life of John Tengo Jabavu*, by DDT Jabavu. I had heard of it, and probably seen it or the spine of its book at home when I was a youngster in my parents' house in the Eastern Cape, before I was carried off to England at the age of thirteen years.

Now, something like 45 years later, I've returned to South Africa for the purpose of writing a biography of my father. On hearing of my presence in RSA and my purpose, someone sent me this mint condition copy, out of the blue. And it is riveting. All of us South Africans should read it, as well as the books I've mentioned.

32

Jazz greats I have known

வூ

10 AUGUST 1977

One of the best parties I ever threw was by chance, as a stand-in hostess. Friends of mine had arranged it in honour of a visiting American Negro jazz musician. (That's what Afro-Americans were called then, so you can roughly calculate the date.)

But at the last minute, a plague of mumps smote their household. The venue was therefore moved to my house. It had been a long time since I'd moved in the jazz world, so for me this unexpected 'do' was something of a departure, a step back to a previous era in my life.

But I was able to keep my end up, I mean, drop names of American jazz giants I had met or had known, such as – I'd better order them alphabetically! – Louis Armstrong, Bill Count Basie, Sidney Bechet, Buck Clayton, Nat King Cole, Duke Ellington, Ella Fitzgerald, Earl Fatha Hines, Teddy Wilson . . .

How on earth had I ever come to rub shoulders with these uncommonly gifted people, these luminaries? Well, I've been married oftener than once or twice, so, you get no marks for guessing it was probably through a husband that such luck came my way! May I whisper a true fact, 'ndinihlebele inyan' nyani'? It is this: a woman gains wonderful experiences through a succession of husbands.

That's why in my heyday I was a believer, bafondini, in the institution of monogamous marriage! However, comes the time when she is old enough to need it no more and can do very well, if not better, on her own.

One of my English husbands had been a jazz impresario, writer, expert on jazz. He wrote in the London jazz papers *Melody Maker*, *Musical Express*; the American magazine *DownBeat*; had his own jazz feature programme on the BBC. And he taught me about jazz and how to write and broadcast my own BBC jazz programmes in turn.

For several years my life was jazz, morning, noon and night. Working trips to jazz gatherings all over England, Paris, Nice. Fascinating, but it exhausted me. Later that husband and I went our separate ways – he to near-millionaire status founding his own recording company, but the friendships he forged for me in the jazz world endure.

You'll notice that the names I've dropped of jazz artistes are those of the 1940s: the 'mainstream' or classical jazz age. Long before bebop, rock, pop, punk. 'Punk' for heaven's sake! That's what it sounds like to classical jazz-trained ears. Mainstream is gentlemanly, cultured, structured. If pop and punk are 'fanakalo, kitchen kaffir*', mainstream is Latin!

For many years jazz lovers in England knew their heroes only from gramophone records (how we treasured our huge collections of precious 78s) because the British Musicians' Union (another of those trade unions) prevented American jazz musicians from performing in England, for fear their superiority would take the bread out of the native musicians' mouths. It was a long battle before the rank and file musicians won against their bureaucratic union leaders, and at last in 1947 the absurd ban was lifted. Our longed-for American jazz gods and goddesses started crossing the Atlantic.

What days those were! I'll never forget the arrival of Duke Ellington and his Orchestra. It was as if the Angel Gabriel and his hosts had descended – a dream come true.

---

* This term is retained in its historic sense in deference to the family's wishes.

A small group of us who were at the nerve centre of England's jazz world at that time called on Duke Ellington by invitation at his hotel – bandleaders, impresarios, journalists. I accompanied my then husband. We were ushered into the Duke's suite.

The great man awaited us, as informal as could be, in a three-quarter length dressing gown, homely bedroom slippers showing bare legs that were coffee brown, long and shapely.

When he had stepped forward to shake my hand first – I was the only lady in the group – with a smile and a bow before greeting the gentlemen, I swore I wouldn't ever wash my hand that had touched that of the genius whom I never imagined I'd meet in the flesh!

He put everyone at ease, chatted away with the utmost grace, affability and authority. I was greatly awed. Presently he paused to instruct an aide to attend to the refreshments. While this was being done amid general chit-chat, he addressed himself courteously to me.

Having been told I was a South African, he said: 'Ain't your country the Alabama, the Mississippi of Africa?' referring of course to the American states that were the most rabidly racist, and went on to ask me about South African black 'ghetto' music, and how the musicians managed. I nearly fainted for I knew nothing about it. My mind not only reeled on being exposed to his, it was utterly blank on the subject of South African black township music. I had nothing to say. What an ignorant fool I felt!

However, on revisiting South Africa in 1976 after a lifetime, I've tried to repair that gap. I've kept my ears wide open to the phenomenon of present-day African urban jazz music makers. As my American friends would say: 'Ah've done pick-up on what the ghetto cats are puttin' down!'

I'll definitely have things to say about it next time I'm asked such as, for instance, the fondness for the electrified guitars, and that 'sound' that comes from juxtaposing harmonium and piano . . . the Americans will 'dig' that, for it's a 'sound' they themselves are fond of in their religious music as well as in their jazz.

I'll play them the records I collected while in South Africa of my favourite vocal groups – especially one led by a growling, gravelly bass that contrasts and alternates with three female voices soprano, alto and mezzo-soprano, close-harmonising in triads, twittering like nightingales.

They'll notice with interest that township music makes less use than they themselves do of transitions, how rarely they modulate, but use other devices by which to alter the fabric of a piece. They'll notice the predilection our ace jazz groups have for the almighty electrification!

My favourite American musician and friend is handsome blue-eyed, brown veteran trumpeter Buck Clayton. When in England he stays with my life-long jazz journalist friends on the *Melody Maker*. When I'm in England, we all gather round my baby grand piano which they bought off me when I emigrated to Kenya eleven years ago. I'll be visiting them again quite soon, coinciding with Buck. There'll be a cocktail party, of course! And I'll drop names this time of South African black jazz men they've not heard of yet.

And I'll have an engaging tale to tell Buck of how, on getting a chance to chat with one splendid black South African trumpeter who, typically, doesn't read music, I asked why he preferred a C Major trumpet to a B Flat trumpet.

The young man turned the instrument over in his hand, examining it as if he'd never seen it before, and considered . . . finally said thoughtfully: 'Well, Auntie Noni, my brother brought it from Cape Town and gave [it to] me. B Flat? C Major? I never asked my brother, Auntie. I just play. It's nice, isn't it?'

What jazz 'cat' could say better than that!

33
Star-spangled bother

❧

17 AUGUST 1977

The printer's ink had scarcely dried on the article I wrote recently about the frustrations my overseas friends and 'extended relatives' and I endured about a year ago when we happened to be in South Africa unexpectedly at the same time, and naturally wanted to meet and spend a night or weekend in the same house which was offered to us by a mutual friend who said: 'Be my guests, darlings; my home is yours and everything in it!'

Some readers of this column wrote, feeling I had been somewhat harsh, and said: 'You would have been allowed to be together in an international five-star hotel, Noni!'

'Well, blow me down!' as some dialects in England have it . . . What sane person prefers staying in hotels, however grand, instead of with mutual friends in a personal private home? Such a person is either insane or ignorant, ijakwa!

And how many individuals of the ordinary income group level can afford this luxury? To be sponsored as a representative of some wealthy company or organisation is one thing. In any case such bodies probably get tax rebates. The generosity they appear to fork out on your behalf isn't necessarily altruistic!

But it's quite another thing for an ordinary person of limited means instead of bottomless purse – umal' iyavuza. You've paid out good money to travel to South Africa in the first place; don't take umbrage if I remind you that South Africa is far from anywhere, is at the outskirts of the civilised world, is beyond the pale – if you catch my double entendre.

Having forced yourself to travel out here for personal reasons, you've budgeted to have some money left over with which to buy gifts for your family, your friends and unexpected new friends or well-wishers … You've done your arithmetic, because on returning home (Kenya in my case), you want to buy presents to take back to demonstrate the beauty and hospitality of your mother country.

Now to be advised that because you're not allowed to spend a night or nights in your friends' house because they are green-complexion and you are yellow, but you are 'allowed' to luxuriate in new-fangled anti-petty apartheid hotels – how far will your limited funds stretch towards those affectionate gifts?

And if your 'multi-national, multi-ethnic' group comprises different sexes, is it unknown that by virtue of the Immorality Act police are empowered to peep through your bedroom keyhole or clamber on ladders to your window to check whether one of the gentlemen in your multi-ethnic party might be kissing goodnight a lady of the same group but of different complexion?

And is it unknown that, although your 'mixed races' group may eat at the same five-star table, they may not waltz or tango together if of dissimilar colours?

This new freedom from petty apartheid of Mr RF Botha's is strictly supervised, believe me. One needs a preliminary orientation course before coming, for South Africa is one of the principal countries in the world where individuals' personal and private actions are controlled by some Big Brother à la George Orwell!

Let me tell you one of my personal experiences of hotels in South – 'Southern' – Africa.

When I was in Natal, two white girlfriends and I arranged to have lunch together in one of these five-stars in Durban at which, being sponsored, one was staying. The other, a South African I'd known years ago in Zanzibar, worked in Durban. She would catch her bus to the hotel. I, being black was staying in a Bantustan location several miles out of the city. (Aren't 'Bantu locations' always absolutely miles out?)

I rode into town on the local (black, of course) bus, having arranged I'd find our South African (white) friend at her office and go by bus with her to the hotel somewhere on the splendid (whites only) beaches. But on reaching my (black) bus terminal, I realised she'd forgotten and I hadn't known that the only bus that goes to the grand areas of five-star hotels is a whites-only bus.

That was all right for her but embarrassing, for what about me, intimate friend of a lifetime? Taxis? I'd have to get a black taxi, change half-way and go on foot, for black taxis couldn't deliver me at the door of the five-star. That area presented unthought of 'ethnic' complications for taxis and their passengers. It was too far to walk in our high heels!

How did I manage, you ask? I nipped around to the offices of my Indian travel agents who had arranged my voyage from Mombasa to Durban, and with whom I'd made friends. They instantly took charge of this ridiculous, inconvenient, humiliating situation. They detailed the driver of one of their personal cars to take me to five-stardom, saying that any time I was ready, he'd come and fetch me back.

Wasn't their action the epitome of sanity, sympathy, kindness? Whenever anyone of any race makes snide remarks to me about Indians or for that matter individual members of any race, my instinct is to punch them on the nose. In an insane world, surely one has to separate one's condemnations of political and human actions...

34
When the sky didn't fall

ঙ্গি

24 AUGUST 1977

Last week I spoke of my experience trying to get to a five-star hotel in Durban. Today I'll talk about hotels in Umtata.

I proceeded there to witness the independence celebrations of Transkei. The hotels which had always been for 'Europeans only' were forthwith decreed open to all races. We 'non-whites' flocked to them out of our pervasive inquisitiveness, to enter these pearly gates, 'to eat and drink alongside Europeans – siyokutya nabelungu!'

For some blacks it was a wonderful, because novel, experience and their surprise was beyond bounds that the skies didn't fall down as they sipped and munched under the stares of their white compatriots.

For others like me, blacks from abroad, the experience was less than wonderful. Indeed, you could say it was an anti-climax.

In Kenya, for example, where I live, apartheid ended long ago, in 1963. Whatever colour your race, you feel as free there on buses, in hotels or restaurants, cinemas, dancehalls, swimming-pools, taxis, night-clubs, churches, as you do anywhere in Europe.

Nobody stares at anyone else – since independence for using public amenities is available. You use those that you can afford. If these say 'informal', that's what they mean. If they say 'tie', then man, you put on tie, mfondini! They even lend you one for your temporary visit if necessary.

Stepping inside my first hotel in Umtata one noon hour to await the opening of shops after their luncheon break, I ordered coffee and sandwiches, meanwhile looking around at the erstwhile 'Europeans Only' paradise.

I found it hideous, 'cheapskate' (as we say in Kenya), vulgar, ill-designed, awkward in the extreme. When the sandwiches finally came, they were not what I had specified. The coffee was cold. I didn't go there again.

After the independence celebrations had ended and the town's hotels had emptied, I moved in from the god-forsaken outlying village, elalini, where I'd been forced to stay temporarily for lack of hotel accommodation. I moved into what was said to be a splendid hotel.

Again, a horrible experience. Hideous, awkward, cheapskate furnishings – like nothing so much as the idea you get on reading a novel set in a low-class boarding or lodging house in England.

'So!' I thought, looking around. 'These are the purlieus South African Europeans had jealously guarded to themselves!'

Next day when I entered the dining-room to take breakfast for the first time, the entire black staff of waitresses – even chefs from the rear, and workmen – gathered in rows at their screen doors to stare at me, this apparition; watched every mouthful I managed to scoop from plate to mouth, watched my Adam's apple as I tried to swallow. I nearly choked – who wouldn't? And left my food unfinished.

The kindly young black housekeeper later apologised on behalf of the establishment, saying that the staff had never before seen or served a black tourist, hence their misbehaviour and rudeness. They were accustomed to serving white tourists. They knew better than to behave towards them as they had done to me. 'Please forgive them, Mama, I've spoken to them.'

I forgave but, nevertheless, moved out with despatch to a different establishment where I was treated with kindness, imagination, even affection as a respected member of the family. I don't know whether that particular hotel – my favourite at Umtata, my home from home – ranks as five-star or not. It certainly does to me – it earned my Award of the Milky Way!

35
How happy in Transkei?

2?s

31 AUGUST 1977

Now that as you know I am no longer in Umtata and environs, I'm
about to fulfil the promise you asked me to make, to write and tell
you 'how happy I was among you there in Transkei Republic'.

Were you not presupposing what I should say in reply? 'Loading
your question', as young people call this kind of request nowadays?
Southern Africans are much like the rest of the world in that they
expect a visitor to adore the country willy-nilly and expect to be
told so. Isn't that the reason you 'load' your request?

Now please don't take offence at what I'm about to say about
this custom or behavioural pattern.

I call it uncivilised!

In France, Switzerland or Trinidad, which are among my favourite countries, nobody ever asked me that. Why not? Because they
don't give a damn. They assume that it's up to you as a private
person to decide whether or not you like living among them. You're
mature, you're an individual, therefore nobody has a right to dic-
tate, pressurise or presuppose whatever inward feelings you may
have in your heart about their way of life or their country.

For example, in France (and in parts of the French-speaking
cantons of Switzerland) we residents don't invite one another into
our houses very much. Not even friends. Our houses are our personal, private kingdoms. I share a flat in Geneva with a white
Kenyan girl-friend – a perfect arrangement. That's how I know

what I'm talking about. She and I like it like this, for we under-stand each other's atavistic backgrounds, and we have shared experiences for over 20 years. I'm on my way there very soon: to breathe again the air of 'freedom, uhuru', after my many months in South Africa.

Now to my personal experiences of my recent life of many months in the Republic of Transkei: yes, I did partly 'enjoy'. Notice this use by Bantu-language speakers of the transitive verb, how they turn it into an intransitive!

At the same time, I did NOT 'enjoy'. I absolutely hated this 'extended family relationship', as it is called technically.

Previously, as a child, I had visited the Transkei only as a young child, a niece of my mother's relatives. My male-mothers, these Gambu brothers and cousin-brothers of hers, made me and her children so welcome! Slaughtered fat sheep for us, so that we might consume the livers. That was our prerogative. We had so many playmates. At that carefree age, did we care who was related to whom? We played, we were sent on errands, and were taught polite manners of Mfengu School people. No mixing with uncivilised red-blankets who used rude language . . .

Half a lifetime later, on coming to Transkei again as an elderly, grey-haired (I wear grey wigs, you know!) lady of nearly 60 years old, my heart overflowed with love towards those of my family whom I knew personally, from my childhood days. At ezilalini/ villages, in the town of Umtata, and in the locations, around about, I found myself surrounded by the approaches of extended 'family' relatives all claiming blood relationship, all claiming it was my duty as the child of their child to take over their responsibilities. These were mainly 'children', and fields to plough and the imple-ments for ploughing.

'Jili omhle!' (That's my respectful, flattering salutation.) 'Jili!

Take this child on my behalf, on your own behalf, and rear him for me and educate him for me so that he may look after me in my old age.'

Inwardly I exclaimed: 'Great Scott!' But kept quiet. After a long silence, every one of us gazing dispiritedly at the mealie patch outside the front door, a very old lady hobbled in supported by a walking stick, pushing a reluctant eight- or nine-year-old in front of her until he and she reached me, to shake my hand. 'Jili omhle, this one I wish to hand to you to take overseas. To educate him, train him, rear him for me, so that he will be my support in my old age.'

I had seen this little boy around for many days – a proper delinquent, neglected, a young thief, a pathological liar. As I had to say something, no matter what, in reply out of Xhosa good manners, I said: 'Aa! Aw! So, it's like that. Whose child is he?'

Answer: 'His mother when she was pregnant with him, was pointed out to me as a member of my clan. Therefore, as soon as she gave birth to the child, this boy, I took him over to look after me when I am old and helpless. But I can't cope now. I am 76 years old, as you know. But you are "related" to this child of mine, so it's for you, please, Jili, to take him away on my behalf.' The old lady hobbled out.

Luckily her snotty-nosed, neglected, mistreated 'child' followed her.

Me? I shall not lift even one finger to help these 'extended' relations.

It's a horrible, uncivilised way of life.

SEPTEMBER

During the month of September only three columns appeared in the *Daily Dispatch*. My hypothesis for the absence of Noni's column on the third Wednesday of September is that it resulted from the death in detention of Stephen Bantu Biko on 12 September 1977.

The second column on 15 September must have been written and programmed for publication probably just before or soon after his death, but before the eruption of nationwide mass protests that ensued when his death became public knowledge. Donald Woods, the editor of the *Daily Dispatch* and a close acquaintance of Biko, was to be banned later in the year as were many South African activists who were imprisoned, banned or banished. The *Daily Dispatch* documented the political upheaval following Biko's death, including the start of the Biko Inquest in October.

Noni's columns for September can be summarised by race, class, inequality and the attendant values of these. Using her experience of living in many countries and her visits to South Africa, Noni writes about her observations, critiquing the practical manifestations of racism – for example, white people who refuse to learn Black people's names because they refuse to call them by their names. To them Black people are the 'despised and rejected'. In this column, 'The despised and rejected', Noni also engages with readers' letters on this topic.

'We Blacks all over the world don't actually have much in common. We can be as different from one another as chalk is from cheese.' This, from the second column 'Message for the rich', was Noni's way of talking about the extended families often seen in Black families. In this discussion she interweaves household labour, its relentless nature and how children – distant relatives – within these extended families end up as 'serfs'. Noni is effectively writing about class among Blacks and how the lines are blurred by blood relations.

The third column also returns to class issues, away from labour to materialism, in 'On peasants and possessions'. She compares her observations of the manifestations of materialism in homes across the countries where she travelled and lived. She views the buying of these material goods as a 'status symbol' and she is clearly disgusted by gaudy material displays.

MAKHOSAZANA XABA

Above: Noni enjoying one of her interests, music, with a friend in the sun. Photograph unmarked and undated. *(Amazwi Museum Collection)*

Willow Cottage, Jamaica, 1962. The note behind the photograph suggests that the photo was taken by Didon Faber (wife of Development Economist, Michael Faber) on a 'Brownie Box' style camera. In the background is one of Noni's other interests, books. *(Amazwi Museum Collection)*

Noni lived in Uganda from 1955, following her visit to South Africa for her brother Tengo's funeral. Here she is seen in the outdoors, explorer-style. *(Amazwi Museum Collection)*

Noni's grandfather was John Tengo Jabavu, a politician, educationist and newspaperman. This group photograph is of members of the Committee of the Inter-State Native College Scheme of which he was a part, and which later became Fort Hare University where Noni was born. From left: JW Weir (Chairman), N MacVicar, KA Hobart Houghton, John Knox Bokwe, JT Jabavu, J Tunyiswa, and seven others. *(Cory Library / Rhodes University / Africa Media Online)*

Left: Sophie Orloff-Davidoff and Noni's grandson, Tengo Carter 'in his (inexperienced) grandmother's arms!' as Noni describes it at the back of the photograph. 10 September 1964. *(Amazwi Museum Collection)*

Right: Margaret, Noni's housekeeper, at age 82, holding her grandson, Tengo and Sophie, 10 September 1964 in Eaton Square. *(Amazwi Museum Collection)*

Noni, Lexie (her sister), Tengo (her nephew), Nicholas and Tengo's Christmas bike, a present from his mother. Christmas 1963 in Jinja, Uganda at Lexie's house. *(Amazwi Museum Collection)*

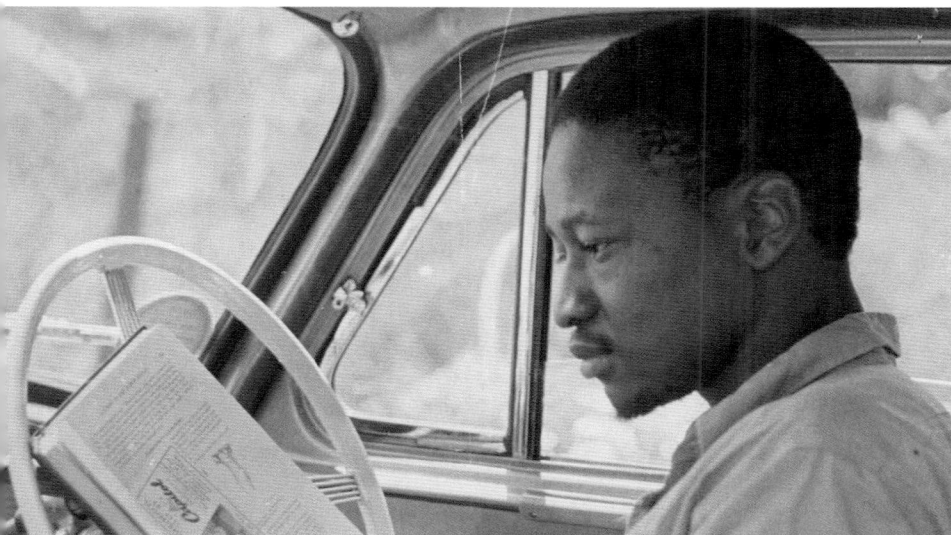

Tengo Max Jabavu, only son of Professor DDT Jabavu and Thandiswa Florence Makiwane and brother to Noni Jabavu. In 1955, he was shot in the head while sitting at the wheel of his car driving from Germiston to Johannesburg. Noni alludes to her trip back to South Africa for his funeral in her columns. He was a final year medical student at Witwatersrand University and was popular among the students and the public alike. *(Baileys African History Archive/Africa Media Online)*

'1960, WC2 London. Kind of sad eh – marriage was breaking up' – Noni's writing at the back of the photograph describing the dissolution of her third marriage. She remained married to Michael Cadbury Crosfield until 1971 but moved to Kenya in 1963. *(Amazwi Museum Collection)*

36
The despised and rejected

๛

7 SEPTEMBER 1977

Do you know that exquisite solo set for mezzo-soprano: 'He was despised and rejected of men; a man of sorrows, and acquainted with grief?' This is a confidently rhetorical question on my part, of course, because since my arrival in 1976 in South Africa after an absence of generations, I became aware again (as when I was young) that practically all South Africans know and love Handel's 'Messiah'. So, I know that your resounding answer will be: 'Yes, and further-more those divine words are Isaiah Chapter 53, third verse.'

I'm opening with these holy words this Wednesday (heathen though I must confess I am!) because every day of every week of every month, year in our country one is bound to encounter a racial insult and, to my mind, such a happening is equal to being 'despised and rejected'.

Our day, yours or mine, may begin with gaiety, a bright dawn, elation, happiness. Then out of the blue, after you've left your humble home you are suddenly refused the service you need and which is your due, and for which you have the money to pay. You find yourself confronted by a scowl, a stare, a refusal. This is a rejection, is it not? You're being treated as less than human. It overwhelms you. And you become 'acquainted with grief'. Your bright day clouds over, for you have been diminished, reduced to a nothing, without having harmed anyone. To collect your senses in such situations is not easy.

It has happened to me from the day I arrived back in my mother country in 1976; has happened repeatedly, and I've written in this column about these unpleasantnesses from time to time when in my indignation, despair, I exploded. Some of you may remember what I wrote about them, in my belief that to share a trouble with others who've been exposed to it, is to halve it.

Today, I want to tell you how so many of you have responded exactly like that. For I know that you will be glad to know. It's not easy for us South Africans to communicate with one another. We are prevented by all sorts of laws, rules, regulations . . .

I received letters about them from the very week I started writing this column, when I had to relate the manner in which I felt 'diminished' as a human being on landing at Jan Smuts airport. An Afrikaner lady 'fell on paper' (as we say in Xhosa about suddenly writing someone a letter):

'Oh Noni, my husband and I read your article and trembled with shame and dismay that a fellow countrywoman was treated like that by one of us. How can we call ourselves civilised? He muttered angrily: "Will they never learn?" Myself, I was at a loss for words. So, I'm writing to say Noni, we're not all alike. In our home we feel hurt by your horrible experience . . . By the way, from the passport details you had to give that immigration boy, you and I are the same age! Please know that so long as you are here in South Africa, we would like to assist you in any way we can, if you would allow us to.'

And she gave me their name, address and telephone number. Later we met and made friends. They invited me to their home for a dinner party in honour of me and my cousin, and I reciprocated by inviting them and some of my friends to a little cocktail party in my hotel suite.

Another letter I got several months later after writing about another such horrible experience was from a young black man, for he addressed me as 'Dear Aunty Noni':

'Listen to what happened at a big chain store yesterday when I was grocering for my mother in Claremont. An African assistant employed there was helping me find things on my mummy's list. An old white guy stumped up and interrupted the assistant. "Hey, John!" The assistant said: "I'm not called John." This old guy became angry and said: "All right then, Peter, what's your name?" The assistant said quietly: "My name is Lennox." The old white guy became furious and shouted: "Do you mean I must ask every boy's name in all these shops?" And he stalked off to find another "boy" to help him find where the article he wanted was stored, which shelf. Aunty Noni, these are our daily encounters.'

These efforts to communicate with me are quite upsetting. To contemplate the cruel situations into which people, children, are forced is truly ghastly*, if I may paraphrase a famous South African phrase which was uttered by someone in authority who usually keeps amazingly quiet on issues that vitally concern all South Africans of whatever complexion.

Some of us whose faces are dark in colour may think it is only we who are 'despised and rejected'. But the correspondence I receive shows me that very many 'non-darks' are also mistreated, diminished, and share the same emotions that we feel. Why? Because they too are human beings.

It's a mistake for us dark ones to think that all whites are cruel. They are not 'all alike'. Many of them, too, are trapped by the authority which dictates what a certain colour person may do or may not do. How can such a society produce happy, natural people? I've been asked this question. Alas, my answer has always been: 'I don't know.'

---

* This refers to former prime minister John Vorster's comment that an alternative to a peaceful settlement for South Africa 'would be too ghastly to contemplate'.

37
Message for the rich

🫖

15 SEPTEMBER 1977

After my lifetime in England, a great part of it spent as a housewife and mother, and then going into other countries again as a house-wife, but only a part-time mother (my children having grown up and left the nest), what took my breath away was the prodigies of housework the black or brown servants are required to do daily.

I was appalled, being by then an Englishwoman 'of the water' as we say in Xhosa. You can say that I have also 'lived' in South Africa as a grown woman since. I spent over a year in South Africa during 1976 and 1977, the country where I was born, but in which I'd spent only my early childhood years.

In South Africa, too, I was appalled to see the amount of work household servants are required to do daily. My observations were so painful that I was tempted either to look away or close my eyes, pricking back tears of sadness for these human beings, but as usual a professional writer had to observe, and register detail.

My observations covered roughly four types of households. These were divisible into social classes – in South Africa, 'ethnicity' classes. These households I experienced, initially as a guest, in the West Indies, North Africa, East Africa and South Africa were of a type in that they belonged to well-off, indeed very rich blacks. I'll begin with these.

We blacks all over the world don't actually have much in common. We can be as different from one another as chalk is from cheese.

164

However, I noticed that we do have in common the sociological phenomenon of what's called an extended family system or remnants of it, a tradition of it, as opposed to what's called a nuclear family system. I am verging on Western sociology, anthropology now which, alas, is suspect among blacks. Many of us suspect that this Western idea of family planning, birth control, is a 'whitey' trick to reduce the numbers of us blacks.

Be that as it may, we seem to believe in 'exploding the population', that children are God's gift. Therefore, our households are normally full to the doorjambs with people, distant relatives, their young people, babies, attendants.

All these, as you well know – talking about South Africa now – are expected to help in the household work. This is part of their training, ukuqeqeshwa. This is the custom, isiko. Romantically, atavistically, isn't it splendid thus to character-train the next generation for their future responsibilities? Indeed, it is, atavistically.

But on the other hand, I noticed that these youngsters, attendants, hangers-on, function as serfs. Paid only in a meal of mealie pap, sugar; if lucky, a few red beans: umngqusho onembotyi. For this, seven days a week, I noticed how they had to turn out, in short spring-clean every room. Take all furniture, rugs, carpets, outdoors to air, wash down walls (thereby misaligning what passed for pictures – no time to straighten these), polish parquet floors, if any, until the surface gleamed like an ice-rink. Then lug everything back indoors and begin dusting! Oh, the dusting method! You had to hit every object (of which the houses are chockful) with a rag. On examining one of these dusting rags, I found that they are filthy dirty. Dust-raising, germ-spreading. What was the point? I was baffled.

In between these Herculean household tasks the servants and young people, being only human, would naturally spend what amounted to hours sitting in the sun, resting, gazing at the view, exchanging gossip at the tops of their vibrant voices. The nephews and male hangers-on would lean on their hoes and rest too. I observed them from my writing work and thought: 'Can they be blamed? The master and mistress of the home will shortly come back from their offices. When they arrive, everybody must be seen to be busy.' The female drudges had to prepare the midday meal for the lord and mistress. The lunch. Mountains of meat, potatoes, whatnot.

East African blacks among whom I now live are not such housework maniacs, buffs. None of this perpetual daily dusting, displacing one's manuscripts, wall-washing, spring-cleaning.

In East Africa, having observed their non-dusting habits, I learned to carry in my handbag my own personal yellow duster with which to surreptitiously wipe the chair I was about to sit on, not so much for the dust, but for chicken droppings. Hens, cockroaches, spiders, ants, fleas, have freedom of the house in the tropics. Why not? Are they not also God's creatures same as we all are – as the Pope says, as the Aga Khan says, as Dominee Vorster says?

However, I've rearranged my life to suit the way I am now in my old age. At home in Nairobi, I employ only three menservants on a part-time basis. They do my rough work, my shopping, my little bits of laundry. No washing off walls, because my walls are lined with books. These they dust with a sucking type of vacuum cleaner, very light to carry. I do my own cooking.

They take turns to do the washing up and not only have they never broken one item of my Wedgwood bone china or crystal glasses, but they get on with their work 'quick quick' (as we say in Swahili) for they know that the Bwana (the lord, master and friend) of their Memsahib (that's me) is liable to appear at any moment to check on how they are treating me.

Swahili is our lingua franca. My servants are Wakamba and don't know a word of English, for they are from the country. They love it when my Bwana comes, for he is a huge Englishman, and their admiration of how he checks their work for me is beyond bounds. He talks with them in an air of tremendous authority about how they must not disturb Memsahib's books, papers, typewriters. And tells them that when he'll be away the following week on business, he expects to return and check that they've done this and that, and not made any household messes.

He checks with me that I'll pay them their money, and not for-get! Money is what they need, we all need, not to be paid in kind or by barter. 'That is past tense, Noni!' And adds: 'I forbid you to overwork these men. If you need extra help and protection – which you always do, so helpless you are – wait until I come. None of this using people as drudges, serfs!' Could this be a message for South Africa's rich?

38

On peasants and possessions

৩৯৫

28 SEPTEMBER 1977

When I came back to Africa to live seriously among Africans in 1951, I was already a grown woman. I had lived in South Africa of course, from birth until the age of thirteen years; doubtless my emotions had been formed by the example and behaviour of my parental environment by the time I was seven years old. That is the Jesuit precept.

I was happy at home, for my parents created a happy household. Beyond that, I can't pretend to have noticed much about how Africans around us lived, least of all how they furnished their homes for we rarely went visiting except to immediate families, Jabavus and Makiwanes, who were the same as us.

But in 1951 I went from England (where I'd lived since thirteen years old) to live in East Africa with one of my previous husbands, an Englishman. Not the other one I spoke of the other week, who introduced me to the classical jazz world. This next husband was a most able documentary film maker. His work took him into the homes of Africans of all walks of life, from the poorest peasants to very rich African landowners indeed, 'saza chiefs' who owned lit-erally hundreds of square miles of territory, through an historic error the British Government made on taking the country under their wing as a Protectorate: they thought that the lands over which the supposed 'chiefs' held sway on behalf of the clan or tribe was the personal private property of the black gentlemen they met.

Mistook them for black landed gentry, and distributed title deeds to them – through interpreters. Therefore, what with the coffee, cotton and other cash crops in which fertile Uganda abounded, these gentry waxed fat and wealthy.

By the time I arrived to live in their country (and I lived there for something like ten years) their descendants owned chauffeur-driven Mercedes Benzes, Rolls Royces (called 'Loi Loi'), wore navy blue suits, shirts, collars and ties, imported brogues – all these under a white Arab-type robe called a 'kanzu', which to me looked like a nightgown – but to be fair, the gentlemen looked dignified in it.

The first time I entered one such a rich man's house, accompanying my then husband who had gone by appointment to arrange filming on a part of his vast lands, the room we were received in was so full of hideous-looking locally made furniture, rickety tables, armchairs and dining chairs, glass-fronted cabinets all lined higgledy-piggledy along the walls, that I thought the inmates were on the point of moving out! Especially as three huge lorries were parked outside the front door, blocking the view of the banana patch.

Household after household I visited was like this one, every item caked with dust and chockful of the most awkward – to my mind – possessions.

Later an expatriate scholar friend at Makerere College, a social scientist from Ecuador, informed me when I asked (I was always asking questions from those I considered to be my peers, professors and such) that 'Peasants are like that'.

'Peasant? But these gentlemen are great landowners, aristocrats,' I said. He explained that it was only over a relatively few decades that Uganda had come into contact with Western civilisation, and its goods and chattels had only recently penetrated into that part of Africa. Not like your South Africa, where you've been in touch with Westernisation for 300 years. When peasants have money and can buy new-fangled goods and chattels, their instinct is to display them, for these are status symbols. And not only in East Africa. Have you ever been in a peasant household in France? I hadn't; had only been in chateaux in the Loire Valley and in fellow-artists' villas in Provence and Menton. My friend gave me a pitying look and justifiably so, for I am indeed ignorant about many things. Well, these status symbols were so uncomfortable, and to my eyes so ugly, that I presently gave up accompanying my then husband on his filming trips.

Came 1976 and I went to South Africa on a long visit, to meet as many of my fellow blacks as possible to hear their news and views of my father, Prof DDT Jabavu, 'uJili', for the purpose of my attempt to write his biography. As his long-absent daughter, I was most hospitably welcomed into people's homes.

As I've said, as a child in South Africa half a century ago, I had rarely been a guest in other people's houses as a family; we had seemed to visit only other members of our families, our close relatives, and of course they lived as we did at home.

So now I was expecting something new in 1976 by visiting people in their homes. To my astonishment, the houses of well-off Africans in South Africa were as chockful as any in East Africa! And, in addition, with equipment: I'd never seen such quantities of possessions! You could hardly move except sideways, crablike, forced to shift a piece of furniture as heavy as lead in order to make progress. Even a side table, coffee table, or dining table – when not in use for a meal – was decorated (if you can call it that) with a frightful doyley crocheted in the shape of butterfly wings. I never saw the piece of furniture which in England we call a 'sofa table' whose purpose is to hold magazines, newspapers, new books currently being read by the inmates of the house. And never saw walls covered with books — the library of the home — as my father's study had been, and my home-from-home in England had been. Was I back in the Uganda of the 1950s?

The only person with whom I could discuss this was a humorous close relative of mine, a wealthy lady doctor of my own age, intanga yam, who had visited England and America on professional trips. We hadn't met in years, but to meet and talk again was as if it was but yesterday. When I mentioned my observations and made comparisons based on what my Ecuadorian social scientist friend had said, she cracked up laughing.

She explained, mopping laughter from her eyes: 'Noni, we are Africans at heart. As for our 300 years of contact with the West, what has it brought us but frustration? So, all we can do is to buy possessions and definitely display them! Every Christmas we change our furniture and buy new — in part exchange, of course. It's competition! If we are seen by neighbours at Christmas without green pantechnicons outside, delivering new stuff, we'd be laughed at; it'll be said we've run out of money!'

I stared, incredulous, and finally said, teasing: 'But one can't take one's earthly possessions to heaven when the time comes, can one? What about the eye of the needle a rich man will be confronted with?' She held her sides laughing her zestful laugh and replied: 'My dear cousin, how ignorant you are! Nowadays there are needle engineers, researching on the production of an elasticised plastic needle, the hole of which will stretch to accommodate our possessions! Because the only heaven we know, we black South Africans, is the next one, up in the sky. We think we deserve it, for what do we have here if not hell?'

OCTOBER

~§

'What else can a writer write about?' is one of the questions Noni poses in response to the question 'Why are you a snob, Noni?' which inspires the first column for October: 'Do you think that I'm a snob?' Noni does not shy away from the accusation of being elitist, as seen throughout her columns and other writings. There is something unnerving about someone like Noni who does not apologise for their experiences. This critique of her snobbery dates to an essay written by Dennis Brutus – 'The New un-African', published in 1962 – lambasting her first book as an example of someone who is not African enough. Noni seems to be shrugging off these sentiments in this column, which is followed by a critique of family life, 'The dangers of family life'. The final paragraph of the column resonates with sentiments popular today about the nature of family dynamics. Some refer to this as Black tax. Noni poses the question which still begs an answer from contemporary readers: 'Friends, you choose; your family is foisted on you if you allow this. And are families not indeed fraught with appalling dangers?'

Noni's preoccupation with the ludicrousness of race relations and apartheid legislation continues in the month of October. She does not hold back from critiquing the apartheid state, which is seen in the title of the column 'When whites hold all the aces'. 'Grappling with the gremlins' presents itself as a column about gremlins such as typos in Noni's writing process; however, she turns this thread

on its head and writes about accents which continue to be an issue
in terms of class and race in South Africa today.

ATHAMBILE MASOLA

39

Do you think that I'm a snob?

❧

5 OCTOBER 1977

Are you a reader of WM Thackeray's novels? I am not particularly, but according to one of my former lovers – now a dear friend – I ought to be. Old Etonians are like that, uptight about what one ought to do, about how one should carry out the responsibilities that accompany one's privileged position in society. He presented me with a rare copy of William Makepeace Thackeray's *The Book of Snobs* and gave me a lecture, saying as he pointed to chapter three: 'Read and digest this: "It is impossible, in our condition of Society, not to be sometimes a Snob."'

My then lover bent down from his great height and bestowed a kiss upon my cheek. It's a long time ago, and those were the days of gallantry and elegance in London. I then reclined on my Mme Récamier sofa, and we had a long chat on the aspects artistic and poetic of 'snobbery' as some people call it, using the word pejoratively.

This incident was over 20 years ago, and I only remembered it during 1976 and 1977, in the months I had to spend in South Africa to meet people who had known my father, the late Prof DDT Jabavu, whose biography I am attempting to write.

Among these people I met an African doctor slightly older than me, whose father – happily 'still with us' as we say in Xhosa, now at a great age – accosted me in the English language: 'My word, Nontando, you are too proud of your father and your mother in your weekly newspaper Wednesday articles.'

I blinked and said nothing in reply, for the accusation baffled me. Fortunately, a blood relative of mine was present, who volunteered an explanation and acted as mediator on seeing I was upset.

He said in English: 'Noni, this statement was not an accusation. It is Xhosarised English. What the doctor meant is that you are justifiably proud of being the child of such great people as your parents were. Everybody is proud of the late "Jili" your father, and the late MaGambu your mother. The entire nation is proud of them. But nowadays when we speak in English, we tend to misuse certain words. Just now when the doctor said you are "too proud" of your late parents, he didn't mean that you are an English snob. I'm about to ask him now, in front of you, to say what he said in Xhosa, to clarify what he meant.'

This was done and the gracious apology that was added, using my clan salutation 'Jili', allayed my hurt feelings. Language is a most delicate, intricate instrument. One has to be very careful indeed in using certain of its words; a literal translation from a thought in one language to a word in another can be misleading, not to say dangerous.

Again in South Africa, on another occasion a friend said to me, I thought belligerently but later found I had mistaken his attitude: 'Why do you write only about professors, dukes, viscountesses, all these upper classes, the elite of the world? Why are you such a snob, Noni?'

By this time, I had gained a measure of control of my reactions to such challenges, and thus was able to say calmly: 'I write and talk only about what I know, about the surroundings I grew up in, where my character was formed. What else can a writer write about? What do you think or suggest I should write about?'

'Why don't you write about the workers of the world, the proletariat, the underprivileged, the have-nots and the pain and deprivations they suffer? After all, you were in World War II in England, and you must have suffered.'

It was a lengthy discussion and here I can only paraphrase what I tried to say in reply: I tried to say that some experiences of pain and suffering, as for example when a woman gives birth to a baby, are tremendous, indescribable, but quickly forgotten – a mechanism of nature's dispensation sees to that.

As to my having been a world's worker during World War II: yes, I indeed did undergo that experience as a young woman. I was not alone in that. My experience was not unique. We world's workers of that time didn't feel deprived. We were well paid. It was an adventure. When it ended, the painful memories faded and were forgotten, as are the pains of giving birth to a child.

What endures in one's mind are the deep-down emotions which were laid down in one's formative years. You can call these 'atavistic'; they may be called nonsense by others. I had no more to say in excuse of my nature, of my writing, of my exultation in my ancestors. If I explain the reason I don't write about the world's workers and underprivileged, it's the truth: I don't know them!

A film star called David Niven (who I'm not acquainted with) wrote in his autobiography that when he was accused of being a 'snob' because he wrote about fellow film stars, directors, producers, instead of the world's workers, such as the chefs and valets who attended his needs when he was a guest in the home of some great Hollywood mogul like Louis B Mayer, he replied:

'Is it not a kind of inverted snobbery to drop names of people you don't know, instead of talking about people whom you did know? I was not intimately acquainted with my host's chefs and valets in Hollywood. They had their job to do and did it splendidly. My presence in the house was because I was the guest of their employer.'

What more can one say, except that as a writer, one can write only about one's own experiences? If they are boring to the reader, he or she is free to turn to another page!

40

The dangers of family life

❧

12 OCTOBER 1977

If what Aldous Huxley said was true – that Henry Ford had been the first to reveal the appalling dangers of family life – then I whole-heartedly agree with the motor car manufacturer. As a child at home, the lives of us kiddywinks may be unalloyed bliss. Not for all of us though, for some of us may be aware of frightful tensions existing between our grown-ups, about which we can do nothing. But mercifully none of us know what the future holds.

For instance, I'm looking at a picture of the beautiful salon, all gold and crimson, in the Vienna Schönbrunn Palace, Room of Millions, in which Marie Antoinette romped and played as a blameless little girl. How was she to know about the seeds of revolution sprouting outside, or that later as a handsome if naive and personable young woman her head would roll, she would be decapitated by the mob for crimes she not only had not committed but was unaware of: 'If, as they say they have no bread, why don't they eat cake?'

I'm also looking at snapshots of my only brother, youngest of our family, and of my elder sister whom I never knew, for she died at two years when I was a four-month-old baby in my pram at Fort Hare. This is a different culture from that in which Marie Antoinette grew up. How was I or my next-born sister (my 'follower' as we say in Bantu languages) to know that our brother when a young man of 26 would be capriciously, senselessly shot dead by a Johannesburg gangster?

As children, we were aware of course that he and I were by no means the favourite children of the family. I was too ugly, endowed with a huge, unbecoming forehead in infancy. My 'follower' (my sister) was so pretty: not only that – she was the replica of my parents' first-born. Now you would imagine that her follower, the youngest and the only son at that, would be the favourite, the best loved.

But for intangible reasons that I will never know, it was not so. He and I were indeed loved, were happy children in a happy home, but our sister was loved more and we accepted the fact, never for a moment resented it. The dispensation of affections within a family is something one cannot argue with, for it can be poetic, another of those intangibles!

As a grown woman returning for a long visit to South Africa my mother country, having brought up a family of my own overseas, I discovered by talking with my few remaining elders that my father had been by no means my grandfather's favourite of his six sons. I was astounded. I'm now talking about a yet different culture. In this Xhosa one, as you may know, the first-born, izibulo, was accorded all available privileges, whether he or she liked it or not.

My father was forced, against his own inclinations, to fill the role his father, John Tengo Jabavu, mapped out for him. He obeyed, and did all that you know he did, to the satisfaction of my grandfather and turned out to be one of South Africa's most splendid men.

However, the more gifted and the most handsome son was my father's next brother, his 'follower', my Uncle Richard Rose Innes. But being 'only' second-born, he had to take second place in the family hierarchy. His gifts, talents, were suppressed. He grew to be a frustrated man, as can be imagined.

In my own case, as another 'only' second-born and never allowed to forget it, I had to fill the shoes of my first-born sister.

Plans for her had of course been mapped out. But after her depature, it became my duty to fulfil them. I've tried. But I suspect I take after my late Uncle Dick in nature, for I'm told in incontrovertible evidence that he was wild. Some who know me well call me 'wild'! They may be correct, for the most difficult thing on earth is to know oneself. Certainly, I'd have preferred to do my 'own thing' (as young people say nowadays). I guess I've done some of them, who knows?

And speaking of cultures, one must remember that they are not static, not granite-like, immovable, as Afrikaner culture has been ordered to be by its rulers. The contiguity of the world's nations – and it's a small world now – causes interaction and change, whether we like it or not.

I can't pretend I've liked some of the changes. These flyovers, this metrification. In Durban, I may as well be in Miami. But everyone to his taste. For instance, during my year in South Africa, I was much pitied by Africans and Afrikaners (their fundamental cultures are surprisingly similar) because I have only two children, one of them my foster child. 'What? Only two? Not even four, or six, or twelve?' I gasped. 'How could I afford to rear, feed, clothe, educate such a multitude? How do you ladies manage?'

Their answers nearly flung me off my chair. One or other would say: 'I've put my middle ones with their uncle, I mean my cousin-brother to look after for me. He is rich.' The custom or tradition seemed to be to distribute one's responsibilities among the extended family. I even met a lady who, when she turned 72 and her offspring had grown up and left the nest, had 'taken' (a sort of unofficial adoption) a boy of 18 months. She felt the need to have a child in the house; someone to send on errands, to weed the mealie patch after school, and who would look after her when she became old and helpless. In short, a little serf, slave, an insurance policy.

My observations over a period of two months was that a delinquent was in process of being manufactured, for at eight years old the child was a pathological liar, a thief, uncontrollable, being thrashed daily. His 'mother', now pushing 80, was in difficulties with him and looking for someone on whom to farm him out, even offered him to me to take abroad and rear for her! I was able to reply truthfully that my teenage grandchildren, in the culture that they were being brought up in, wouldn't like it. Too hazardous a venture. They had their own playmates and a little serf, slave, wouldn't fit in among their friends.

Friends you choose; your family is foisted on you if you allow this. And are families not indeed fraught with appalling dangers?

41

Grappling with the gremlins

ॐ

21 OCTOBER 1977

May I tell you today who constitute the enemies of anyone who writes newspaper columns? They are not mainly among yourselves, dear readers. Some among you have faults that annoy a columnist, and I intend to mention them presently for your edification, that in capital letters, you are LAZY, NINGAMAVILA, NINENTLONI! But first listen to what I have to tell you about enemies of writers . . .

These are gremlins who secretly and invisibly enter your typewriter as you prepare the fair copy of your article; they make a mess in it, thus puzzle your readers. And again, at the production stage of the newspaper, these gremlins interfere with the fingers of the skilled men who set the type and make messes of their work.

Who are these gremlins? In our Xhosa language, we call them ootikoloshe, and describe them as mischievous creatures. In Irish English they are called hobgoblins. Each is described as a 'naughty, small, man-like creature, possessing a prehensile tail, horns on his head and teeth set wide apart, amazinyo-agqagqeneyo'.

I've never met anyone who claims to have seen a tikoloshe, gremlin, hobgoblin. Yet the belief in his existence is pervasive, however imaginary. And I confess that I, too, am a believer!

Why? Well, for instance a few Wednesdays ago, I wrote about how my grandsons in England would react on hearing the South African English accents of Eastern Cape whites and would laugh at what they'd consider an 'oddity' of these Albany district accents.

Now a gremlin or tikoloshe interfered and excised the entire lines which were most important, explanatory, and germane to the subject. I had written that these young English speakers of aristocratic, affected tones would laugh, because they'd say: 'But grandma,' (that's what they call me) 'this isn't Cockney. Is it of Devonian or Cornish or Geordie descent?'

By 'Geordie' they'd mean the English accent of north-eastern England which, because of centuries of connection with Scandinavian mariners, is noticeably influenced by the Scandinavian accent, tone and lilt.

As you know, the Cape Province also had historical contacts with mariners from England – mostly from the West of England, Devon, Cornwall – and of course Brittany, France. The surname 'Le Breton', for example, is not an uncommon one in Cornwall . . .

In the Eastern Cape 'settler country' – 'amaSetlani' these people were mostly from the West of England, Devon, Cornwall and so on. Their descendants speak a type of English which derives from their ancestors. There's absolutely nothing wrong or despicable about it. Not only is it charming in many ways to new ears, but linguistically it is most educative, believe me! And its history grips your imagination.

But my grandsons (I mean 'my English ones'), who inherit Xhosa or rather Mfengu genes as well as English genes (amalawana wam, my young mixed-blood descendants) from the elite families they belong to in South Africa and England, are going through their phase of rebellion against 'old fogey' authority.

They move in elite society in the UK and are trying to express their own personalities; what parent hasn't experienced this phenomenon? So, they like to speak in a Cockney accent, just to annoy and baffle their three grandparents, myself who lives thousands of miles away abroad and visits them only rarely and their other two who are English and live in England, and whom obviously they visit more often.

When I'm there and hear my grandsons talk 'Cockney English' with their aristocratic playmates, I keep quiet. For in English upper-class society, a grandmother is forbidden by custom to interfere or make suggestions to her children's upbringing of their children, her descendants. It's not 'black' society in which matters are done differently.

Let me share part of a letter I received the other day after that article about South African Eastern Cape accents from a white lady who teaches English in an open school:

'It was most interesting to see how my class reacted to your column, trying to face the fact that their own English may sound uncultured or strange to other ears. I'm glad to say that after some thought, they chortled among themselves and then admitted to me that they "really learn something from Noni and wouldn't miss her Wednesday articles for anything!" I understand they are composing a letter to you.'

I find this most moving . . .

Now to you, my age mates, zintanga zam', my tydgenoot, when I started off by accusing you of being lazy, why is it that only our young ones of all South African 'ethnic' groups read books and write letters? Are you elderly ones perhaps grappling with gremlins?

42

When whites hold all the aces

🍵

26 OCTOBER 1977

When I was on my recent long visit to South Africa after an absence of generations from my mother country, various matters impressed themselves on my mind and made me happy or unhappy. I'm about to talk about two of these today.

But first I must begin, according to our polite Xhosa custom, by according a courtesy towards all of you who were my hosts and welcomed me into your homes in my capacity as 'intombi kaJili', daughter of the man whose clan salutation was 'Jili' and whom you respect to this day long after he left us. The courtesy among Nguni peoples is that when a visitor is about to depart is proposing to leave your house, he or she has 'to ask permission to ask for the road'.

You may have spent hour after hour calling on your hosts, watched them sending children – little serfs – and young relatives and servants running in all directions back and forth, or to catch household chickens to pluck and cook with which to feed you, their honoured guest. In my case, the child of their honoured great man. By thus treating me, they were honouring him, my grand-father, splendid man of Africa, let alone of South Africa. I was shining in his brilliant light.

During those hours my mind tended to be occupied by ancillary items. Being brought up from childhood abroad as an English-woman, I found I couldn't absorb too much of the repetitiousness of Xhosa-language conversation. I tended at times to listen to it with only half an ear.

One day as we sat chatting and admiring one another, sincokola sibukana, the FM radio on full blast, I heard a reported speech by someone called Prof Van Zyl of the University of the Orange Free State. He was reported as having said: 'Bantu homelands have regional planning. So why can't the white heartland of South Africa also have regional planning?'

Those two words 'white heartland' were arresting to my foreign ears. So, I asked my hosts: 'What does this Professor mean by white heartlands? Is a heart white anyway? And what does he mean by its lands? Isn't a heart an organ inside the body, anatomically speaking? Or is he talking about a game of cards, hearts and spades?'

My hosts exchanged wry smiles, saying nothing in reply. I got the message. 'Walls have ears.' So, reverting to my own thoughts and interpretations of anatomy, biology, physiology, clinical medicine and such, I realised that these disciplines are compartmented, in South Africa of nowadays, into separate groups – racial, ethnic. The heartland of South Africa is that vast tract of our country which may belong only to those of our fellow countrymen who are nowadays legally labelled as 'white' in complexion, with the privileges that go with South African 'whiteness' of complexion.

I asked myself: what does this Prof Van Zyl mean? Myself, I've never clapped eyes on a 'white' person. Even an albino is not 'white'. I've been happily married overseas to some 'white' men. They were not what I'd call 'white'. Neither they nor my in-laws regarded me as 'black'.

My descendants from those unions – who have grown to be very jolly teenagers at expensive boarding schools overseas – are not regarded by me or their grandparents or uncles and aunts and cousins as 'ethnic'. That South African Government vogue word is unknown outside South Africa. My descendants are regarded and treated as human beings, whatever their personalities may be (and in all families, everyone is different).

While I was figuring all these thoughts out, and of course politely waiting for my hosts to 'give me the road, permission to leave them', I remembered to inquire of them: 'All these education systems, Bantu Education, Coloured Education, Indian Education, run by gentlemen with Afrikaans names – who runs "white" education in present-day South Africa?'

They smiled and answered: 'There isn't one. He is the Minister of NATIONAL Education.' I was stunned and kept quiet while I munched away at the food they had so graciously put before me – doubtless depriving themselves in honour of the families of which I was a descendant. At last I murmured, more to myself than them, to save them from embarrassment: 'In short, the best things in South African life are for those who are legally labelled "white". Everything else, which is necessarily of inferior quality, is for those who are legally labelled "non-white". Those who are in power and rule the country may label anything by whatever colour ethnic label they like. Theirs is the power to declare that "unequal facilities are equal."'

In silence, I asked myself: 'Where now, Lord Acton, with your highly quotable dictum (has it been translated into the local African language or Afrikaans, by the way?): "Power tends to corrupt, and absolute power corrupts absolutely" ... I wonder if you ever played cards, crap, and held all the aces in your hand?'

NOVEMBER

Born in March in the same year as Noni, the world-renowned pianist and vocalist Nat King Cole was Noni's friend. Noni opened her first column 'Let there be love' by sharing an experience in London when Nat King Cole sang and made the 'notoriously reticent audience' go 'wild', writing how he and his trio went to Noni's house afterwards for a meal. Noni used Nat King Cole's song 'Please let there be love' to make connections between music and poetry as both artistic genres tend to meditate on love in this 'unjust world …'

In the second column, 'The good news and the bad news', Noni continues to write about the South Africa that made her 'very unhappy' during her visit. She comments on the numerous contradictory statements that were being issued by the apartheid regime and how these made her think she might be 'insane'. She writes about taking time to listen to the various radio stations and the music they played. She applauds the expertise of 'black announcers' on SABC radio:

> When the Black announcers are allowed to stop giving out the official government propaganda which masquerades as 'news', and can relax and do what's called in the free world 'ad-libbing' which means chat between themselves and make jokes about non-political and innocuous topics, these Black men and women are among the finest, most expert I have heard. (And me, I am an expert!)

Noni continues to tackle the theme of diversity in the third and fifth columns. While the third column is focused on history, the fifth is about her personal experiences as a 'Stranger at home'. In the column on 'Flight of the amaMfengu', Noni shares her understanding of the history of her family, how the Jabavu people were descendants from Natal. They were part of those who fled from the wars that King Shaka led in the 18th century in his pursuit of building a Zulu nation. This column veers towards the topic of nationalism in various settings, and Noni shares her experiences as a foreign national in the various countries where she lived. While Noni centres language as an aspect of diversity in the final column, her mobility is indelibly entwined in her writing. In the fourth column, 'What's in a name?', Noni writes about her fascination with the names people are given at birth.

MAKHOSAZANA XABA

43

Let there be love

ඥ

2 NOVEMBER 1977

Are you an admirer of that musical giant artist, the late Nat King
Cole, pianist, singer, bandleader? You may not know that he was
in addition a tall, slim, handsome jet-black American, endowed
with the most endearing smile, courteous beyond belief. He died
at an early age – a fact which not everyone knows, for although he
was not in search of immortalising his name, he has become an
immortal through his artistry.

He was one of my friends; his daughter Natalie, also a most gifted
singer, was – and probably still is – a friend of a daughter of mine.
Whether Nat's and my grandchildren are also friends, I don't know.
Some families and friends are scattered nowadays, live and travel
in different continents and we have to accept that our lives are
our own.

Nathaniel Cole was one of those whom the gods admire and
therefore decide to remove from the scene of this horrible world . . .
so Nat was 'taken from us, wasishiya' (as we say in Xhosa) at the
young age of 42.

His memory, his presence lives on, even in racist countries which
suppress that he was black in complexion. The young who play his
records sometimes don't even know that he was a black man, blackest of the black. They don't care, bless their young hearts!

One of my favourite records that Nat and his trio made way back
in the early 1940s and which is available and bought in great

numbers even in South Africa, is a small one of the size I think called a '47 LP'. It is 'Please Let There Be Love'. How charmingly Nat sings, how beautifully and expertly he and his trio accompany the song!

When they performed in a concert hall to their packed audiences, they were turned out in midnight blue suits. These made them look blacker, more beautiful. The technicians had of course arranged the technicalities beforehand for the tympanists and for Nat – his piano had to be of a certain make, the tension of the keys had to be right for his touch, his stool had to be adjusted in such a way that he could swivel at will, while playing, to keep contact with his audience. For had they not paid good money to come enjoy being with him?

'Please Let There Be Love.' The night he sang that, the audience went wild, was transported. It was a British audience, notoriously reticent, as you know. The hall wasn't far from my house. So later, Nat and his trio came round to my house to eat and relax and talk.

Among other pieces of music, we talked about 'Let There Be Love', with my grandson, a babe, in my arms in my Belgravia house. Nat and his companions dutifully admired him, realising that a grand-mother is as proud of her grandchild as their own 'grands' had been of them as infants. Presently, they rose and went over to my piano and performed for their own pleasure. I listened; so did my grandson.

But in my mind, I was thinking of the universal emotions about love which Nat had aroused in the normally reticent British audience in the concert hall shortly before and not far away. Nat had raised love to the plateau to which it rightly belongs: its rarefied, cloudless, inspiring atmosphere. Inspiration is the only word for it.

Some people say that love makes the world go round or turns you on. They may be right. In my personal opinion, much of this is a debasement, a degradation of an emotion, a part of life I think of as elevated.

To hear Nat sing his 'Please Let There Be Love' – his American accent makes it sound like Pleeze Let Thair Be Lerve – is to feel yourself elevated. Nat made the ditty into poetry.

Are you familiar with the works of John Donne, the 17th-century English poet? Or with the poetry of Robert Graves, contemporary English poet who is happily still with us, at a great age now? RG is another friend of mine (am I not fortunate in my friendships? Accidents of birth).

John Donne tended to write about unrequited love: 'The dawn breaks not/Tis my heart' (sic) . . . I wasn't aware of the meaning of this until the son of an English scholar, a specialist on John Donne, pointed out to me his father's works on Donne. The son, one of my lovers (of long ago, of course), an Old Etonian, introduced me to poetry, especially to the works of John Keats – another one whom the gods loved and therefore took in extreme youth from this unjust world . . . Shelley? Byron – a selfish, handsome beast if ever there was one! Nat King Cole was not my lover in any sense of the word. He was one of the rare civilised men who understood and could abide by the philosophy of fidelity to his wife, and understood the meaning of a platonic friendship between a man and a woman, as does Robert Graves.

Africans, Afrikaners, be they of peasant or pastoral background, are as yet to be at loggerheads about the 'message' of this 20th century and its 'coloured' Cubans, Russians, Chinese, Japanese, knocking at the Cape of Storms.

What idiocy changed the name to Cape of Good Hope? As an old lady, I cling for comfort in my remaining years to the ditty of my late friend Nat King Cole, 'Pleeze Let Thair Be Lerve' . . .

44
The good news and the bad news

During my lifetime abroad, I became a broadcasting and television personality, a 'star'. Gave talks, read plays, participated in discussions and all that. On television, I was quite presentable, for I was pretty, good-looking, photogenic in those days! Past tense!

Naturally during my many months here in South Africa, on my visit which has to end soon according to the immigration laws, I've paid some attention to South African broadcasting. Your FM, your Zulu, Xhosa, Afrikaans, English programmes. And although I've been very unhappy here, I hope to tell you some good news about my experiences of listening to your South African broadcasts.

Let me start by what I consider the bad news, the nasty. I mean the 'news'. So-called news. It's not what's known as 'news' in the free world. It's only official propaganda, immediately followed by an exultant announcement – 'rugby!' or 'tennis!', 'cricket!' ... Upon which a sane person switches off. I consider myself to be sane but by now, after 15 months in South Africa, maybe I'm insane, for I can't make head or tail of the contradictory statements emanating from your rulers, your powers that be. On the radio, they make me dizzy. None of its right hands seem to know what its left hands are doing.

So, forget them. Let's talk about good news now!

While I was in South Africa, I greatly enjoyed the classical music broadcast on your Afrikaans ethnic programme: Beethoven, Bach,

193

Dvorak, Handel, Haydn, Mendelssohn, Ralph Vaughan Williams (who by the way is a cousin of mine by one of my marriages). 'Late' now, of course, but I'm proud indeed to belong to such a galaxy of uncommon, gifted people.

On your white SABC programmes, I've found the talks about books inspiring and interestingly presented. I've been overjoyed to listen again to BBC programmes of half a century ago – The Goon Show, My Word, Tony Hancock, Mr Glum.

Your South African 'white' comic programmes confuse me, for I can't catch the meanings of your Van der Merwes or boerewors or biltong. Obviously, these are local, parochial. An outsider, a person of the world, can't be expected to follow languages like Afrikaans, unless he or she has Afrikaans or Afrikaner atavistic feelings. These atavistic feelings are totally logical and poetic. Nothing wrong with them. Some of my very best friends are Afrikaners – they don't take offence when I refer to them as 'boers', as they were called in my childhood, 'farmers'.

In Kenya, we call the descendants of those boers who trekked up to East Africa 'kaburu'. Again, not a swear word. Some of our black people's best friends up there in Kenya are 'kaburu'. This ethnicity is something we don't understand or even want to.

So now back to your black ethnic SABC programmes. Good news! When the black announcers are allowed to stop giving out the official government propaganda which masquerades as 'news', and can relax and do what's called in the free world 'ad-libbing', which means chat between themselves and make jokes about non-political, innocuous topics, these black men and women are among the finest, most expert I have ever heard. (And me, I'm an expert!) They sound natural, spontaneous. Why? Because they've worked on their material beforehand, have done their homework. How else could they make their public cheerful, happy?

45
Flight of the amaMfengu

৩৫

Of course, all of you dear readers of this column are aware that my parents, the late Jili and the late MaGambu, were amaMfengu. Their forefathers derived from southern Natal, a place now called Harding.

Many people had to flee from their homes, leave their cattle behind, and some lost children. Why? Because of the Imfecane, the scattering of people resulting from the military domination and wars of King Shaka during the 18th century.

A section of Zulu people fled south, as far down as Peddie, Grahamstown, Alice and Tyume. These regions were already occupied by Xhosa people. The Xhosa were a hospitable people. Their king gave us permission to settle among them, despite our 'tsefula' language, as serfs. We were poor, had no cattle. We were amaMfengu (milkers of their cows). We had no property, we had nothing. We were serfs.

But serfs, immigrants, make great efforts to establish themselves in order that their children may be respected; the condition of being a serf, a refugee is not comfortable. We Mfengus did what other refugees all over the world do. Ask Americans whether they like having West Indians, Puerto Ricans, Mexicans among them. Then ask Malawians or Tanzanians whether they like having South Africans living among them. You may or may not be surprised by the answer you will get. Generally, the hosts who at first pity and sympathise with the refugees later don't like them too much. Why? Because they become 'too active, and don't remain as serfs'. Refugees rise from this condition, buy land, become farmers, businessmen for the sake of their progeny and thus become suspect, disliked by the local nationals. I discovered that we Mfengus are not much liked by the Xhosa people nowadays because some of us became active, ambitious (as refugees tend to be) and took to education. Descendants of Jabavu and Makiwane and Bikitsha are examples. I discovered as a member of Jabavu and Makiwane descendants that we are not liked much by the Gcaleka people nowadays.

I myself find it difficult to mix with 'refugees' from South Africa. In fact, I forbid them to visit my little flat in Nairobi. Why? Because I've found them to be social delinquents. They even steal your soap, your cigarettes, your matches. They seem to think the world owes them a living. Is this attitude not romanticism? Or am I mistaken? Many years ago, I read a book called *The Romantic Exiles* by EH Carr. It isn't 'banned' or classified as 'undesirable literature' in South Africa and is quite cheap, a paperback. It is about the lives of Russian elites who fled Russia because they hated serfdom under the Tsars, and also hated communism, Trotskyism, hated military dictatorship.

Perhaps my Mfengu progenitors were of the same type, and perhaps that's why they fled, became scattered up and down Africa when Shaka established his military regime.

During the 1950s, I visited the countries which were then called Southern Rhodesia, Nyasaland, on my way to Uganda and Italy. Can you imagine my amazement when I was visited by descendants of amaMfengu who had fled north during the Imfecane? I was only a passer-by, but news spread that a daughter of the Professor was around. So, people came to pay their respects, not to me personally, but as a representative of Professor Jabavu.

And in Kenya where I now live, there were more astonishments for me. AmaMfengu whose progenitors had trekked up there as servants of their Boers (kaburu, which in Swahili is not a designation of hatred but a word of affection), came to my hotel when I happened to be on a visit to the Highlands. People came in swarms to visit me because I am the daughter of my father. These people were amaMfengu. How they heard of my presence, I'll never know. Bush telegraph, perhaps? Like ancient Greeks, they came 'bearing gifts and wine' to convey their sympathy for the death of the only son of the Professor, the Ntlangwini Professor they so respected, of the Ntlangwinis who had fled south during the Imfecane caused by Shaka. Of course, we could talk only in Kikuyu and Swahili for, understandably, after three generations you lose the facility of your mother tongue.

The visitors brought chicken (live, feet bound) and a sheep to be slaughtered before my eyes, the liver and intestines to be cleaned there and then, for me to eat. It was their symbol of sympathy for the death of my father's only son. Fortunately, the hotel people were from the Comoro Islands and therefore spoke French, English, Swahili and understood the customs. I had to look away while the slaughtering was going on. Customs are different, aren't they? One has to be flexible!

46
What's in a name?

❧

If you think I've forgotten or abandoned my 'Book of Collected South African Babies' Names', you are mistaken. I'm working at it all the time and I promise myself that it's the most enjoyable book I'll ever write, for the contents are at hand, ready-made as it were. I don't have to THINK about them as one does when writing one's usual book. Of course, I'll have to 'think' when I edit, page-proof, copy. But when that time comes, even such names I'll have to eventually exclude are to me interesting and mystifying and give me food for thought in my old age. By the way it was my 58th birthday recently, bendibhaafa! (This is another phrase, a transliteration which is enormously interesting to a linguist – I'll talk about it another Wednesday).

Back to my book about South African babies' names ... During the many months I spent in South Africa between 1976 and 1977, I noticed that the boy's name 'Jody' seems to be popular among white ('waat') South Africans. I had never heard it among 'white ethnics' in the countries I have lived in. And while I was in South Africa, nobody could explain its origin or derivation! So, I'll have to exclude it from my *Book of South African Babies' Names*, because it's not good for a writer to write about matters outside her personal knowledge.

But I was personally introduced to a little 'black ethnic' girl aged about twelve whose name was 'Gloriosa'. I exclaimed to her mother:

'But that's not an English language name!' The young mother replied with calm and dignity and charm, addressing me as 'Auntie' (out of respect for my age): 'Her full baptismal name is Gloriosa Superba'. I was open-mouthed with surprise. My astonishment was so great that I'm afraid I cross-examined the lady: 'How did you parents come to give your daughter this Latin name?'

I am no Latinist but as you all know my father, uJili, was a Latinist. I can 'hear' (as we say in Xhosa and other languages) the difference between Latin and English ... the reply was lengthy. Every detail has to be gone into and explained, kufuneka kuhlakulwe! So, I must paraphrase, and must remind you that these cross-examinations are not resented in our culture: they are expected, welcomed because we are deeply interested in other people, in human relationships and, time being endless, we can talk by the hour about them. Actually, not all of us blacks in the world are like South African blacks ... in the Western world, the West Indies, the Americas, we call it CPT which means Coloured People Time: but I'll tell you about that on another Wednesday.

The explanation about Gloriosa's baptismal name was – to paraphrase it – that when her mother was a domestic worker in Natal and became pregnant, her employer ('my Madam') was interested in flowers, iiblomtjies ... in other words I gathered she was a botanist, and suggested this name to be bestowed upon the young one on his or her arrival: 'Flame Lily'. The parents had no idea why, but the Madam was so 'kind, humane, so nice to them', that they acted on her suggestion.

Gloriosa Superba looked down on the ground while her mother and I talked. Out of respect for her elders. In any case, she wasn't expected to participate in their conversation about her. At last – it must have seemed like ages to her – I held out my hand in greeting to her and said 'Kuboni!' her paternal clan name. She greeted me also and smiled, shyly, as she held the hand of this new 'Auntie'.

A name I'll not exclude from my *Book of South African Babies'*
Names is that of a small black boy, 'Galaxy'. How poetic, how
imaginative, I thought. The universe. The stars.

But on hearing the explanation I felt surprised, even let down, for
his parents knew nothing about stars, the Milky Way, the Southern
Cross. The splendid name had been bestowed upon him because
the day he was born, his father acquired a second-hand motor car,
unomaxesha of that trade name.

When I spoke of the stars, of galaxies, they stared at me as if I
were crazy, and said: 'Those are always there. Why for us to bother
looking at them? But a material possession like a motor car, now
that is an important event. Our son is proud of his name, although
here at home we call him by his other name. Bless his little heart!'
He looked on the ground, because he was not included in the conversation about him. Respect for his old people.

47
Stranger at home

30 NOVEMBER 1977

Now that the time has come for me to prepare to leave South Africa and go home, I find myself being asked the same questions as I was asked when I arrived. 'Why don't you stay with us, Jili?' (To help non-Xhosa speakers, 'Jili' is my paternal clan salutation; as a woman, I'm really 'Ma Jili', female gender. But to honour my late father, I am saluted as 'Jili', the male gender. And I glow with pleasure. Who wouldn't? For it shows the love and respect with which my father is held, even though he 'left us, died' so long ago. (August 4 1959, to be exact) . . .

My reply has to be 'Kaloku, a woman has to be at emzini wakhe, the home she married into'. I came to South Africa in order to carry out the duty of collecting material about my father's life's work so as to write his biography. I've been down here for over a year doing this work. But as a woman, I am needed at my home for I've been away for too long. My people there need me.'

Perhaps I reply in old-fashioned, atavistic Xhosa language, for I am a Swahili and Kikuyu and Nandi and Kisii speaker nowadays. For when I reply, my cross-examiners stare at me in wonder. Perhaps I stare at them too. I don't know, except that I feel my eyes becoming open and round during the cross-examination, for I think to myself: 'Why should I leave home? In what respect am I needed down here in South Africa?' Inwardly, I begin to suspect that my courteous cross-examiners are 'talking just for the sake of talking, bathetha nje'! I've been away from South Africa for so long that I don't understand your customs, and I've noticed that you don't seem to understand mine either. Who should be blamed, or why blame anyone? Isn't life like that? Shouldn't we all accept one another as we are? Of course, one cannot accept criminals and murderers: what I mean is that South Africa is so full of variety, it is a pity to separate its inhabitants by force, by law. We all have such cultural riches to exchange with one another! When 'apartheid' is lifted, we don't lose our identities at all – it is simply lovely to talk to one another about our historical backgrounds, our forefathers, our beliefs, our family training, the way we live. I say this from personal experiences which I am about to relate now – if you don't mind!

For instance, although I can say much about Italy, Spain, the West Indies, USA, North and East Africa, when it comes to South Africa where I was born, I find that I can't say much about Natal. I would have only unpleasant things to say about that region, although my ancestors originated from there. As for Durban, 'Durbs', I had better say nothing. I was forced to stay there for many weeks and wasn't happy or at ease, for reasons which might not interest you. But I must tell you one of them: I don't speak Zulu, so although I was among educated people who could communicate with me in the English language, they spoke only in the Zulu language. Thus, I was left out and couldn't participate. As a Xhosa speaker, I seemed to be a sort of leper. So, I had to say 'Goodnight, everyone', and retire to my room.

I felt unhappy, unwanted, not needed. Who wouldn't, in such a situation? Everyone there respected and loved my late father Professor Jabavu and his wife MaGambu and had therefore invited me, their daughter. But they had not imagined that after 40 years abroad, I might be different from my parents whom they had admired. But isn't each child in a family 'different' from either its parents and/

or siblings? Therefore, like anyone else, I am 'different'. As you know, my father was a Latinist and expert in South-Eastern Bantu Languages. Me, I'm 'different' because I have a working knowledge of East African Bantu languages and French. The only South-Eastern Bantu Language I know and can speak is Xhosa of the old-fashioned type. Oh my – the orthography! This has been changed over and over since I was a child. So, like everyone else, I find it better to write in the world language, the English language. My doing so creates accusations that I am 'too European, ndingumlungukazi'! I found this accusation difficult to understand. And it made me unhappy. After all, doesn't a child speak as others around him or her? So, is it my fault that I speak Xhosa of 40 years ago? And that on being sent to England at the tender age of thirteen I acquired the English tone, their way of speaking? This tone? Can I help it?

My own grandchildren – I have four – speak in their own accents: British and American. When I visit them, it fascinates me to hear them talk with their young friends. And it seems to fascinate them too to hear their grandmother talk with her accent. They always ask me to talk and teach them in Xhosa, Swahili, Kikuyu, Nandi, Kisii. I try but I ask them, the little giants (they are much taller than me), to teach me their own accents. And guess what? They immediately run outside to play! Children are like that all over the world I suppose, in not enjoying being asked by their grandparents to teach them anything. But when you reach the age of 58, which I have, you forget how you felt at the age of eighteen!

Anyway, I visited Umtata. When I bumped into people in the street, they exclaimed. 'Yuini, nanku uNoni'. 'Goodness, that must be Noni,' using my first name because they had seen the drawing of me in the paper, of my hands. Then we would talk and they politely adjusted their address and called me 'Auntie Noni'.

Well-brought up children. Another Wednesday I'll talk about the well-brought-up young Afrikaners I met in Grahamstown and Cape Town. My admiration for you of all races who live here is beyond bounds. For me it has been hard, difficult, uncomfortable; but not your fault! You were on the whole very kind and welcoming to a black foreigner. Imagine, I count as a foreigner now, although I was born in South Africa nearly 60 years ago! But things were different in those days. South Africa was a Dominion of the British Empire, and everyone was free to be friends. Among my parents' friends were such people as Lord Athlone, Dr Abdurhaman, Lord Clarendon, General Smuts. I was too young to know them myself at that time. I only observed in my childish way the people who used to visit my parents.

Some of them still remain in my memory, such as the linguist Prof Peter Lestrade, a specialist in the Sesuthu language, and Chief Tshekedi Khama. Such people are historical now and may mean nothing to the present generation. So, I won't talk about them. Another Wednesday, I'll talk about the young people of your own generation whom I met when I was invited to Grahamstown.

DECEMBER

❧

In December Noni seems to be more reflective of her time in South Africa. In the column 'Happiness at Rhodes' she reflects on her stint spent visiting Rhodes University, while doing research for a book about her father. I suspect Noni would disagree with those who refer to this university as UCKAR: University-Currently-Known-As-Rhodes. She would not share their sentiments of Rhodes being an exclusionary space for Black students. Her time spent at Rhodes lingers with nostalgia, as it reminds Noni of her childhood spent at the University of Fort Hare.

The reflections continue with a column about language and accents as well as a comparison of her trip to Cape Agulhas – the southernmost tip of the continent 'owona wona mzantsi Afrika' – with her trip to Cape Bon, Tunisia, 'the northernmost eyona yona ntla Afrika'. It seems that Noni cannot write about travel without writing about race, as the column is infused with musings on racial segregation as she has experienced it in other countries on the continent. The reflection ends with a question still relevant today insofar as protectionism amongst white South Africans is concerned, which lingers from apartheid legislation: 'What is apartheid protecting South African whites from?'

ATHAMBILE MASOLA

48

Happiness at Rhodes

usς

7 DECEMBER 1977

People in general in South Africa want to know as much as possible about a stranger, and don't mind asking you point-blank personal questions! At first, I was puzzled that blacks down here should behave like this for in the many black countries I've lived in, people are the opposite. Particularly in East Africa where I've lived for nearly 20 years, partly in Kenya, partly in Uganda. There, people don't greet one another as they do down here, let alone ask one another personal questions such as 'Who are you, where are you going and why – are you married, where is your husband, how many children have you got?' In the West Indies, the Americas, Canada also, people don't greet one another.

On thinking the matter over, I wondered: 'Could it be the psychological background of slavery, oppression in those countries?' (I even met actual slaves in Uganda when I lived there during the 1950s!) But I doubt if I'm correct for when I was asked: 'Where were you happiest in South Africa?' I had to reply, 'At Rhodes University and Grahamstown.'

To begin with I felt awkward at Rhodes University, because after having stayed for several months in Zululand and then Transkei and being accustomed to this greeting business, I found it strange that on meeting on the campus roads the young people, students, teenagers abantwana avoided your eyes, looked the other way. Indeed, the first person who spontaneously said 'Hello' to me on the campus was a little girl of seven or eight years. I suppose at that age you are unaware of the politics of race and colour. After all, who is looking after you at home? It's usually a black lady. You probably even play with children whose colour you don't notice. It's when you get bigger that you are forbidden to play with such little friends and are instructed that they are the 'wrong' colour.

Anyway, I was happy on Rhodes campus I suppose because I was born on one, at Fort Hare. The Rhodes students looked different though, wearing jeans, hair flowing. Those I remembered at Fort Hare about 50 years ago had worn Oxford bags, ties, Stetson hats, and the women students had worn dresses. Nowadays, I couldn't differentiate the boys from the girls. Unisex?

But I greatly admired their noiselessness. For instance, they never revved the engines of their motor cars, or made noise when they threw parties. They seemed to respect the need for other people to sleep at night. How different from Umtata. The noise there? Indescribable. I suppose because I wasn't accustomed to it.

However, after I'd been around on Rhodes University campus for a few weeks and had given a couple of lectures, students and citizens began to approach me – even came to my cottage uninvited, to chat with me and my Makiwane first cousin. I had sent for her from Umtata to keep me company and as a holiday for her.

My visitors didn't come just out of nosiness. Some were from the Transvaal, Orange Free State, Cape Town and had never been to Transkei, let alone Kenya, Mexico or the West Indies. They interested me as much as I seemed to interest them. Young or old, they were very well mannered. They were interested to hear about the countries I've lived in, and I was interested to hear about theirs. I was greatly touched when two white girls, students of about nineteen or twenty, stopped me and said: 'Excuse us please – what time is it? Our watches have stopped.'

Improbable! But I realised it was their way of making contact with someone of a different race.

Isn't it sad that South Africans are so separated and prevented by all sorts of laws from meeting one another?

But perhaps changes will be made. Mr Vorster said so in one of his rare but powerful orations.

49
Far different north

14 DECEMBER 1977

Although my protracted visit to South Africa after so long away –
Rip Van Winkle – has been so packed with shocks that some of my
best friends among you are declaring that my brain seems to be
getting addled, this visit has nevertheless afforded me some
immense pleasure.

Perhaps because I'm one of those who are determined to be happy,
no matter what!

But you may be correct, my friends, in saying my mind may be
getting confused; I don't deny it, although I hope you are only
teasing me as I tease you sometimes . . . You've no idea what it feels
like to be in an apartheid land when you aren't used to it. Even the
southern states of the USA were better by the time I visited them
in the late 1960s.

But I hope you won't think I'm totally crazy today in telling you
that my greatest pleasure has been my achievement of a long-
standing ambition – to visit the 'southernmost tip of Africa owona
wona mzantsi Afrika'!

I've nurtured this wish ever since, many years ago, I visited the
northernmost eyona yona ntla Afrika, which as I don't need to tell
you learned ones is Cap Bon, Tunisia, if you remember your geography of school days. When I was a girl at Lovedale Practising School
up to 1933, we used to call that lesson 'joe graphy'.

I had been sent to Tunis to write some articles for two distinguished British newspapers, the London *Sunday Telegraph* and the then *Manchester Guardian*. While there, in order to give me a break from staying at my hotel, a French girlfriend of mine, Jeanine, and her Tunisian Arab husband, Rachid Driss, Ambassador of Tunisia to the United States, invited me to their weekend cottage at Cap Bon for a few days.

How thrilled I was to be shown the remains, the ruins of buildings the Romans had erected on colonising the Mediterranean lands, of which North Africa was one, centuries ago BC, the then known world! Carthage for instance. 'Cartago' as the locals pronounce it.

You felt yourself breathing the air of ancient cultural backgrounds. And how I wished I were a Latinist! Would you believe that I, granddaughter of a lover of Latin, John Tengo Jabavu, daughter of a veritable Professor of Latin, DDT Jabavu, who imparted the language to hundreds of you learned ones, was never taught a word of it? Isn't that a case of 'shoemaker's daughter the worst shod'?

But a process of symbiosis must work, for I have learnt to manage somehow; because to see as I did all around me that the people of northernmost Africa are mostly brown, indistinguishable from coloured in South African parlance, and some white and quite a number jet black, all of them possible descendants of the 'miscegenation' (again South African parlance) of Romans and freed slaves and Arabs, was to remember that Roman colonisers were considerably more enlightened than subsequent colonisers of Africa.

For one thing, they didn't practise a colour bar, a white consciousness. Slavery yes, of course. Slaves were white (the little British, English ones, *'Non angli, sed Angeli'* – remember?) as well as black.

But wasn't Roman slavery better than ethnic grouping by force? A slave of whatever colour had the political right on gaining freedom, whatever his complexion, to join the ranks of the citizenry. *Civis Romanus sum.*

Romans were colour-blind. Their culture indeed had its aspects of mercilessness, vulgarity for don't forget, they were not Christians, let alone a 'bastion of Western Christian civilisation'.

You Latinists among my readers can tell me which of the Caesars of the Roman Empire was a man of African descent, can't you?

Thus, there's no apartheid at Cap Bon, no racially demarcated bits of beach. Anyone can swim or live where he likes. My French friend, her Arab husband and their brown son and I, black guest, didn't have to separate according to colour and group.

Places of worship were open to all. Next-door villas, studios, bungalows, cottages, belonged to people of any colour. Whites get so sun-tanned anyway, you can't tell them from Arabs or browns.

These thoughts returned to my mind as I and my Western Cape brown friends who had taken me to Cape Agulhas disported ourselves — illegally — at my longed-for southernmost point of our vast continent. All around I beheld weekend cottages, villas, studios, places of worship which are, of course, for 'whites only'.

People of other complexions may not build themselves anything like that there. Indeed 'non-whites' — the brown, coloured people, descendants of Khoikhoi and Holland Dutch in this part of the world — have perforce to dwell in 'locations', out of sight of the salubrious areas that have been designated 'whites only'.

As I clambered onto the Needles (as the rock formation is called there), I couldn't help comparing southernmost with northernmost.

During our drive to Cape Agulhas, passing through the most beautiful rolling wheatlands you could ever imagine, we lost the way once or twice, and unexpectedly came upon remote white farmhouses and asked for directions. The white ethnic farmer ladies who ran to the gate to speak to us (it is obviously a very lonely life in these parts) wearing aprons and broken farm shoes put me in mind of 'hillbilly' white farmer women I had espied in Tennessee, let alone in the backwoods of West Virginia, USA, regions which metropolitan Americans describe as 'backward beyond recall' and even in more spectacular terms. Read your HL Mencken.

I realised I was gazing upon 'Afrikaner ethnic cultural backgrounds'. And a thought entered my mind: 'Wouldn't southernmost Africa have been fortunate had it been colonised, like northernmost Africa, by the Romans?'

Up at Cap Bon – in Tunisia generally, come to that – I had been overwhelmed by that wonderful sensation of freedom, equal opportunity, mutual respect among peoples.

All right, Nero had fiddled while Rome burned but look out, scholars are bringing evidence on which we must re-evaluate even Nero.

I'm not sure how to describe the sensations that overwhelmed me on gazing round down at Cape Agulhas and environs. Such 'cultural ruins' as I saw were a few pathetic fishermen's cottages, etc, some of which are being restored and declared National Monuments. Such whites-only villas, cottages as I saw put me in mind of those I had seen around the Great Lakes regions in Canada, which were referred to by my Bostonian or Upstate New York friends as 'low class'. (They meant 'not in the same league as Hyannis Port and such!')

My feelings at Cape Agulhas were in turmoil: were they of freedom, equal opportunity, mutual respect among peoples? Or should I re-evaluate the cultural heritage of this part of Africa according to the manner in which it was spelt out, for instance, by Messrs Eiselen and Verwoerd into 'apartheid'?

What is apartheid protecting South African whites from? Did the Romans feel a need to 'protect' their Virgils, Ovids and Ciceros from contamination by contiguity to people of different complexions?

Or are you telling me the truth, my reader friends, when you declare: 'Noni, people like you can never understand what our South African apartheid stands for. Its glorious meaning is beyond you. It may addle your brain if you try to make comparisons!'

50

How to learn from your ears

ॐ

The telephone can be a teacher, even a party line here in South Africa. I learned a lesson in an amusing manner one day on the telephone during this protracted visit to my mother country.

I rang up one of my new friends (I've been lucky enough to make friends across colour or class lines). This new friend is an English-speaking white. She and her husband had invited me to dine with them and friends at their house a few nights before. The children of the house, two young boys not yet teenagers, had been introduced. They kept absolutely quiet, just staring at me with rounded eyes, as if registering me, never to be forgotten – the way children do.

So now I rang up their mother, giving my name. The younger boy answered. Then I heard him call out: 'Mummy!,' and tell her who wanted to speak to her. He repeated my words as I had uttered them, but in a highly exaggerated imitation of my accent, and laughing his little head off. I now realised that the stares he and his brother had subjected me to had been because they'd been concentrating their little ears on my unusual accent. I smiled. By the time my friend, his mother, came on the line I was laughing helplessly.

And as I told her how I had heard her son laughing about my accent and imitating it, I added: 'Tell him to hold his hand over the receiver, another time!' She too fell down laughing – who wouldn't? Her young son had made our day.

Children's ears are so quick to detect and pick up any form of speech, unaware that they are exercising a most amazing skill. This little South African English-speaking young chap didn't know that he had detected differences in pronunciation between my overseas-English speech and his South African-English speech which grown-up linguists, professors, elocutionists, write whole books about in analysing them.

Chapters of their treaties are illustrated by diagrams of palatal positions of the tongue, teeth, epiglottis, trachea, ribcages, intakes and expellings of breath, positions of lungs. Other chapters outline the historical backgrounds of the various English language accents, the pronunciation phenomena that this language shows all over the world, not only here in South Africa but in Australia, Wales, Canada, Ireland, USA – any land where English is either the only or the main, or a second language.

I myself had not been very much aware of South African English as spoken here by English-speaking South Africans. Not until my present long visit. Before I was sent to England as a child, I'd been surrounded on Fort Hare Native College campus where I was born by black English speakers. My parents' neighbours – my father's white fellow professors – were either 'English' English speakers, or 'Scots' English speakers. Similarly, at Lovedale Missionary Institution which I attended as a daygirl from Sub-Std A up to Std V in 1933. We children used to have fun imitating our teachers' accents behind their backs. I'd completely forgotten this, until my new friend's young son's acting on the telephone reminded me.

On being taken to England to live with my English guardians and go to school there, my guardians and their relations and friends were of one social class. Like a child I forgot about South African English. I noticed it only occasionally, when for instance Oom Jannie, die Oubaas, Gen Smuts, came to stay with us. He spoke English in a strong Afrikaans accent. And in his jolly way, when he saw me and the other children in the house staring at him silently, he teased us by exaggerating his Boer accent.

When World War II broke out, I was a young adult in England and was called up for war work. I began to meet native English speakers of different social classes from my own: aristocratic young women (I was only upper middle class); working-class women; women from farms – agricultural types – women from every region of England, from Devon, Norfolk, Sutherland, Lancashire. We all teased one another mercilessly, making fun of our varying accents!

After the war and later as a full-grown adult, married, a mother and so on, the horizons of my experiences of hearing English widened considerably for my life took me to live as a settler in many different countries. For instance in the West Indies; I lived there long enough to be able to detect the pronunciations of Trinidadians, Barbadians, Antiguans and so on, as compared with, say, Jamaicans. On every island, the people use and speak their mother tongue (which of course is English) differently. Accents derive from historical backgrounds. As descendants of slaves, much depends on what nationality the former slave owners had been – English, Welsh, Scots, whatever. Again, I participated with islanders in teasing and joking with West Indians of other islands about their accents!

Then in the USA where I lived and worked for some time, what an engaging multiplicity of accents! I liked best the English that Southerners speak – soft, mellifluous, lilting, heavily influenced by the way Southern black Americans speak. Blacks are in the majority in 'Dixie' as they affectionately call those states south of the Mason-Dixon Line . . .

Travelling as I had to almost all over the United States and Canada, I was often in difficulties, for my 'English' English was a nine days' wonder . . . as were American regional accents to me. Again much joking, teasing, staring at one another as we tried to understand our funny-peculiar accents!

Then later on, as an oldish woman – ewe kaloku, ndimdala bafondini! There's no denying that I am old, my friends! I returned to Africa, to live in Kenya. Again, surrounded by African speakers of English, blacks being in the majority of course, as everywhere in Africa. I had no linguistic problems with my 'white' Kenya friends, because Kenya whites mostly belong to the social class I grew up in in England, that's to say upper middle class and aristocrats. (England is like that, bound by the social class system!)

But I had to learn Swahili until fluent. After that, learn to distinguish between the accents of black speakers-of-English. At first, they all sounded the same to me. But gradually I became able to tell whether a black English speaker was Kikuyu, JaLuo, Nandi, M'Kamba, Masai or whatever. At last I felt I had arrived, had graduated as it were! To them, I sound like a 'mzungu, European, umlungu'. All over East and Southern Africa, in the countries I have visited – the then Tanganyika, the then Rhodesias, the then Nyasaland – the really fluent English speakers were Nyasalanders, Malawians. They have a linguistic background of Scots English teachers. Scottish missionaries were very correct in speaking and imparting the English language.

Now in my old age, I'm back in my mother country, surrounded by the black majority population. My ears – in their second childhood now! – have noticed the various accents in the various areas I've visited in this vast land.

I get the impression that in South Africa, during my absence of over two generations – behind my back as it were – the 'English' English, 'Scots' English, 'Cockney' English, have given way to, or been crushed down by an Afrikaans, a 'Boer' pronunciation of English. And English is now something like a second language!

I've found myself having to positively stare at local white South African English speakers, for example in shops, offices, bottle stores or banks, and talking to travel agents, immigration officers and so on, because I couldn't at first understand them. It was only after my friend's young son unwittingly opened my ears that I realised that my very own accent is difficult to understand when local South African whites first hear me! So, they stare! I had ascribed these stares to hostility. But was I perhaps mistaken? Were we not outstaring one another in an effort to understand each other's speech? Not always because we hated one another's complexions because of apartheid?

Well, isn't it nice that little children can open the eyes of their big people, their elders, as my friend's young son did on the telephone, and how he made all of us laugh and be happy! Does this event make you feel happy, as it makes me feel; that the future of our lovely South Africa may be safer in the hands of the young ones? So many of them are struggling in their juvenile way to put our country to rights. Nothing that happens here, as they grow up, 'leaves them cold'*.

---

* This refers to the comment 'It leaves me cold' that the then Minister of Police, Jimmy Kruger, made about the death of Steve Biko.

Afterword

꧁

This book represents a high point in my journey with Noni Jabavu. I first read about her in 2009 when I began writing for the *Daily Dispatch*. I was a student at the time and writing for the *Daily Dispatch* was a milestone for a young woman living in the small student town. I had grown up reading the newspaper with my dad on Saturday mornings. While he read the first half of the paper I would begin with 'The Chiel', which was a quirky section with riddles and literary musings (it has since been replaced by the opinion and analysis section). We would swap sections and I would read the news as well. I never imagined that one day my writing would appear in the same newspaper, as well as other national newspapers such as the *Mail and Guardian* and the *Sunday Independent*. Writing the columns was an opportunity for me to think out loud, but also see myself as a part of the broader public discourse. But I felt a sense of unease because people were responding to me as though I was exceptional, as there were so few Black women occupying the public discourse and opinion pages at the time. I wanted to see my writing as part of a broader conversation with other women writers. Discovering that Noni Jabavu had also written columns for the same newspaper more than 40 years before me opened a door to questions about her erasure.

When I started writing for the *Daily Dispatch*, I remember reading the works of Nomalanga Mkhize, Nomboniso Gasa and the late Kazeka Mashologu as some of the Black women who were contributing to the opinion pages in newspapers. The fact that I cannot recall many other names of Black women journalists requires a deeper look into the archives and poses difficult questions about the nature of erasure or absence alluded to in the introduction.

My unease led me to ask questions: why were there so few Black women writers in my curriculum? Where were Black women's voices being heard? It wasn't good enough for me that most Black women found expression in church, as I had seen in my childhood. I wanted to know the spectrum of women's involvement in public life. I began to google 'Black South African women writers'. It was a furious quest fuelled by a feverish desperation. Noni Jabavu emerged in one of my searches and I breathed a sigh of relief. Soon after I found a copy of *Women Writing Africa*, a four-part anthology series which confirmed my hunch: Black women have been writing and participating in the public discourse for centuries, but the colonial and patriarchal framework in my education refused to acknowledge or see these women's voices as valuable. During my honours year a friend of mine introduced me to Nontsizi Mgqwetho's poetry from the 1920s newspaper *Umteteli wa Bantu*. Nontsizi's poetry was renewed when it was compiled into the book *The Nation's Bounty* and, in the same way, Noni's words have also been renewed into a book rather than being buried in an old newspaper.

Even though I was finding names and snippets of writing by Black women, something was still missing. I knew that Noni had written two books, but they were not available in bookstores I visited. It was as though I had imagined them into being. I eventually found a copy of *The Ochre People* by mistake in a library at a monastery on the edge of Makhanda while on a visit for a writing retreat. It felt as though I had found Noni in the flesh. It was only years later that I could find copies of both of Noni's books in what felt like a serendipitous moment in an antique bookstore in

Johannesburg. Finding the books felt like an invitation from Noni that I could not refuse: read my work and bring me out of obscurity. Since then I have been writing about other Black women writers and women who occupied the public discourse. Makhosazana mentioned the research I did of the *Bantu World*, which is a start to more explorations and writing I hope to do. I hope to write about Frieda Bokwe Matthews' writing in the same newspaper alongside Rilda Marta, as their writing is an example of how women wrote about the ways in which they occupied the world. Rilda Marta's letter, in which she wrote about her trip to America, appeared in 1935 and Mrs Matthews wrote about her trip to London – where she includes an anecdote about meeting young Noni on this trip – in a letter which is a reflection for her readers. Like Noni's writing, these women's work offers an image of the kind of worlds in which women lived beyond the narrow prescriptions Makhosazana mentions.

My favourite column, 'Smuts and I', published in February, demonstrates the complex nature of Noni's life. What did it mean for a young preteen girl to refer to General Jan Smuts as 'Oom Jannie' and describe him as a 'Jolly old man, he talked non-stop'? Noni describes her childhood as being characterised by 'non-racial friendliness and contacts between its resident Boers, English, natives – such names as Taylor, Glass, Burl, Tremeer, Jabavu, Bokwe and so on'. This seems counter-intuitive to the grand narrative about race relations in early 20th-century South Africa. It is both surprising and unsurprising that the views she shares about race are still pervasive today in conversations about race relations in South Africa. And this is the beauty of this book: Noni's writing gives us a glimpse into the past; a past which continues to linger in the present. Her writing about the importance of reading is still relevant today and the once wildly successful Abantu Book Festival is an answer to Noni's questions about the nature of reading culture in Black communities. When I consider the current debates about race relations and class, Noni's writing seems particularly poignant. When I see the expanse of gated communities and securitised complexes in the suburbs and I hear about the racism which continues unabated in schools that retain a white majority, I am reminded of the question she poses in the column 'Far different north' in December: 'What is apartheid protecting South African whites from?' Today the question still begs: what are white South Africans protecting themselves from?

Her writing about 'The ochre people of Transkei' is another example of the exploration of the past which offers us perspectives about the present. Like her book *The Ochre People* (1963), this article is an exploration of Noni's relationship with amaqaba – those who continue to use ochre and resist Westernisation – as someone who comes from an elite, educated family. This exploration is captured in the question 'But I asked myself, why do I never see "Christian, school people" talking to our beautiful ochre people?' There is something existential in this question when read in the context of students demanding a decolonised education in current-day South Africa. How will decolonisation happen if those who are educated in the hallowed halls of universities are not in conversation with those outside the academy who may have the answers?

In 2018 I was asked to teach *The Ochre People* to first-year students at Wits University. It was a difficult feat, given that students only had access to a PDF version of the book. Many decided not to print the book out, so I don't know how many students eventually read it. Judging by the exam essays which I received – fewer than ten. This experience demonstrates the need for this book as well as the reprint of Noni's previous two books. It should become required reading in journalism and literary studies departments in order to bring Noni's voice out of obscurity in a format that students can see, feel, touch and hear.

This book is an intentional calling of Noni's name in order to resist the intellectual erasure of her work. In her book *Beyond Respectability: The intellectual thought of race women,* Brittney Cooper writes about the intellectual work of African American women in the 19th and 20th centuries. In the same way that African American intellectual history would fall apart at the seams without the voices of Black women, South Africa's intellectual history and knowledge production would unravel if we did not remember the work of Black women included in the introduction as well as those mentioned above. The African American women Cooper writes about would compile lists of women's names in various publications to catalogue their achievements. Cooper explains these lists as 'Their own genealogies of Black women thinkers. I do not think of these lists as mere lists. Instead the intentional calling of names created an intellectual genealogy of raced women's work and was a practice of resistance against intellectual erasure.' Cooper refers to this as listing and it is worth quoting her at length:

> These lists situate Black women within a long lineage of prior women who have done similar kinds of work, and naming those women grants intellectual, political, and/or cultural legitimacy to the Black women speaking their names. Listing also refers in the fashion industry to an edge produced on a piece of fabric and applied to a seam to prevent it from unravelling. In similar fashion, Black women's long traditions of intellectual production constitute a critical edge, without which the broader history of African American knowledge production would unravel and come apart at the seams.[23]

Without an engagement with Noni's work and Black women journalists from the past, the current work and contributions by other essay writers and journalists seem out of context rather than in conversation with writers from the past.

Noni is part of the legacy of Black women writers in South Africa. More importantly, the cohort of young Black women writers who have become more visible post-1994 are also part of Noni's story. Literary ancestors like Noni Jabavu, Daisy Makiwane, Charlotte Maxeke, Nontsizi Mgqwetho, Frieda Bokwe Matthews, Ellen Pumla Ngozwana, Lauretta Ngcobo, Miriam Tlali, Ellen Kuzwayo, Lilian Tshabalala, Adelaide Tantsi, Mina Soga and many others whose names are yet to emerge enrich the story of what it means to be a woman who crosses borders and disrupts public discourse through her writing.

These women wrote themselves into history and we owe it to ourselves to pay attention to their stories and their voices in the way that this book has done. The silences and gaps about them raise questions about the archives: who remains in newspaper archives and remains unseen? There are some books which have used newspaper archives from the early 20th century, but the authors have mostly been men: SEK Mqhayi, Isaac Wauchope and William Gqoba, with Nontsizi Mgqwetho being the only woman whose work has been resuscitated. We need to go back to the papers as a literary archive and actively look for women's names; I suspect we will be shocked by what we'll find.

There are three voices representing three generations in this work: Noni Jabavu's, Makhosazana Xaba's and mine. This intergenerational, multi-vocality makes it a unique collection as it places Noni Jabavu's work in conversation with the work Makhosazana and I do. Through our research on Noni Jabavu, Makhosazana and I have spent hours talking about the need to resist the erasure and silencing of women's voices. As a poet and editor of many books, Makhosazana's oeuvre is an example of how she resists erasure and she has been an inspiring companion on the journey towards the production of this book. She has also produced an anthology of literary critique, personal essays and interviews *Our Words, Our Worlds: Writing on Black South African Women Poets, 2000-2018* (UKZN Press, 2019) which is a celebration of Black women's writing. This book is yet another celebration which we hope will spur on more books which resist erasure and the silencing of women's voices.

ATHAMBILE MASOLA

Endnotes

1. Nicolette Louw (Ferreira). MA Thesis. Grace and The Townships Housewife: Excavating South African Black women's magazines from the 1960s. https://scholar.sun.ac.za/bitstream/handle/10019.1/4064/louw_grace_2009.pdf? Last accessed 12/02/2019.

2. Nicolette Ferreira (2011) Grace and the Townships Housewife: Excavating black South African women's magazines from the 1960s, *Agenda* 25:4, 59-68, DOI:10.1080/10130950.2011.630558.

3. Ibid.

4. Ibid.

5. Nicolette Louw (Ferreira). MA Thesis. Grace and The Townships Housewife: Excavating South African Black women's magazines from the 1960s. https://scholar.sun.ac.za/bitstream/handle/10019.1/4064/louw_grace_2009.pdf? Last accessed 12/02/2019.

6. Ibid., p. 187.

7. Ibid., p. 186.

8. Ibid., p. 187.

9. Williams, G. The history of the Daily Dispatch. https://www.dispatchlive.co.za/history/. Last accessed 07/02/2019.

10. Jabavu, N. 12 January 1977. Back home again. *Daily Dispatch*, p. 8.

11. Sarita Ranchod. Stories on Karima Brown, Sophie Tema, Ferial Haffajee and Joyce Sikhakhane in *Herstories Celebrating Pioneering Women in South African Journalism*. http://www.rjr.ru.ac.za/rjrpdf/rjr_no24/herstories.pdf. Last accessed 6/02/2019.

12. Gaele Sobott-Mogwe, Interview with Juby Mayet, Johannesburg, 29 July 1993 in *Journal of Gender Studies*, 3 (1994). https://www.tandfonline.com/doi/pdf/10.1080/09589236.1994.9960582?Last accessed 6/02/2019.

13. Meg Samuelson (Hamsie Kathleen Jeffreys). 2003. Though I am Black I am Comely in Woman Writing Africa. The Southern Region. M.J. Daymond, Dorothy Driver, Sheila Meintjies, Lebola Molema, Chiedza Musengezi, Margie Orford and Nobantu Rasebotsa (eds). Wits University Press, Johannesburg, p. 229.

14. Ntongela Masilela Charlotte Mannya Maxeke. 2003. Social Conditions Among Bantu Women and Girls in Woman Writing Africa. The Southern Region. M.J. Daymond, Dorothy Driver, Sheila Meintjies, Lebola Molema, Chiedza Musengezi, Margie Orford and Nobantu Rasebotsa (eds). Wits University Press, Johannesburg, p. 195.

15 Berrian, B. *Bibliography of African Women Writers and Journalists* (Ancient Egypt – 1984). Three Continents Press: Washington, DC, p. 104–112.

16 Ibid.

17 Masola, A. Bantu women on the move: Black women and the politics of identity in the Bantu World, *Historia* 63, 1 May 2018, p. 93–111. http://dx.doi.org/10.17159/2309-8392/2018/v63n1a5. Last accessed 6/2/2019.

18 Ibid.

19 Dube, J. You Go Girl. Herstories Celebrating Pioneering Women in South African Journalism. http://www.rjr.ru.ac.za/rjrpdf/rjr_no24/herstories.pdf. Last accessed 6/02/2019.

20 Peterson, B., Mkhize, K. & Xaba, M. (eds). (2022) *African Foundational Writers: Peter Abrahams, Noni Jabavu, Sibusiso Nyembezi & Eskia Mphahlele*. Wits University Press.

21 Masola A. (2022) A Footnote and a Pioneer: Noni Jabavu's Legacy. In: Peterson, B., Mkhize, K. & Xaba, M. (eds). *African Foundational Writers: Peter Abrahams, Noni Jabavu, Sibusiso Nyembezi & Eskia Mphahlele*. Wits University Press, p. 95-115

22 Xaba M. (2022) "She Certainly Couldn't Be Conventional If She Tried": Noni Jabavu, the Editor of *The New Strand* Magazine in London. In: Peterson, B., Mkhize, K. & Xaba, M. (eds). *African Foundational Writers: Peter Abrahams, Noni Jabavu, Sibusiso Nyembezi & Eskia Mphahlele*. Wits University Press, p. 355-376

23 Cooper, Brittney C. (2017) *Beyond Respectability: The Intellectual Thought of Race Women*. University of Illinois Press.

About the compilers

MAKHOSAZANA XABA is an anthologist, essayist, short story writer and poet. She has published numerous biographical fragments and academic essays on Noni Jabavu including two tributes published soon after Noni's death. Xaba's 2006 MA thesis, 'Jabavu's Journey' includes three biographical chapters on Noni's life and the most recent chapter appears in a 2022 volume *African Foundational Writers: Peter Abrahams, Noni Jabavu, Sibusiso Nyembezi & Eskia Mphahlele* edited by Bhekizizwe Peterson, Khwezi Mkhize and Makhosazana Xaba.

She has pioneered research and writerly activism on Noni Jabavu for almost two decades, thus reigniting awareness and interest in Noni's writings and life. Xaba is currently a visiting professor of practice in the Humanities Faculty at UJ.

ATHAMBILE MASOLA is a writer, researcher, poet and teacher at the University of Cape Town. She has a PhD from Rhodes University which focuses on black women's historiography, intellectual histories and life writing with a focus on Noni Jabavu and Sisonke Msimang's memoirs. Together with Xolisa Guzula, she is the co-author of a history series for children: *Imbokodo: women who shape us* which profiles 30 women's micro-histories (Jacana Media, 2022). Her debut collection of poems, *Ilifa*, is written in isiXhosa and published by uHlanga Press in 2021. The collection was the co-winner of the NIHSS Award for Best Fiction (Poetry) in 2022. She is a Mandela-Rhodes Scholar (2010).

Her writing has been published in a variety of academic publications as well as magazines and newspapers such as *Prufrock*, *Sable Literary Magazine*, *Al Jazeera*, *Mail and Guardian* and *The Sunday Times*.